the economics of
Public Issues

Seventh Edition

Douglass C. North
WASHINGTON UNIVERSITY, ST. LOUIS

Roger LeRoy Miller
CLEMSON UNIVERSITY

1817

HARPER & ROW, PUBLISHERS, New York
Cambridge, Philadelphia, San Francisco, Washington
London, Mexico City, São Paulo, Singapore, Sydney

R. L. M. dedicates this edition to
Steven J. Hendlin

Thanks for your help.

Sponsoring Editor: John Greenman
Project Coordination: R. David Newcomer Associates
Cover Illustration and Design: Pencil Point Studio
Compositor: Auto-Graphics, Inc.
Printer and Binder: The Malloy Lithographing Company

THE ECONOMICS OF PUBLIC ISSUES, Seventh Edition

87 88 89 90   9 8 7 6 5 4 3 2 1

Contents

Preface

Economists cannot tell people what they ought to do. They can only expose the costs and benefits of various alternatives so that citizens in a democratic society can make better choices. In this book, we present the interested reader with some ideas of what the costs and benefits are for various proposed social actions. Economic issues surround us in our daily lives, in our work and in our play. Often, we may not even be aware of the extent to which economics affects public issues. Nonetheless, it plays a large role in most public issues, whether we are talking about water, illegal drugs, crime prevention, higher education, or professional sports.

For students first taking an introductory economics course, this book is offered as a supplement to the main text. Reading it in conjunction with a book that explains economic theory in detail can demonstrate both the relevance of that theory and the way in which it can be used to analyze the world around us. No previously acquired knowledge of economics is necessary for understanding any of the chapters in this book. Necessarily, then, the reader must be warned that in no case is our treatment of a topic exhaustive. We have merely attempted to expose the bare economic bones of some aspects of the issues treated. Further class discussion will undoubtedly reveal the more complex nature of those issues.

The seventh edition has been updated in every respect. In addition, we have examined some new issues of current interest: The Economics of Staying Alive at 55 MPH (Chapter 3); The Economics of the High Cost of Alcohol (Chapter 12); The Economics of Cutthroat Pricing (Chapter 13); The Economics of Comparable Worth (Chapter 14); The Economics of Women and Divorce (Chapter 15); The Economics of More Taxes and Less Work (Chapter 19); and The Economics of Housing Prices and Controlling Growth (Chapter 26).

Teaching economic theory by way of current issues continues to prove effective for many instructors. The new issues that we have chosen, we believe, will continue to keep students interested in microeconomic analysis.

This book includes a set of pedagogical devices to help the student reader better understand the economic analysis that applies to each part and chapter. These devices are as follows:

1. An introductory explanation precedes each of the five parts. Where applicable, economic terms are set in boldface in these sections.
2. Economic terms are set in boldface the first time they appear in the text. All boldface terms are defined in a glossary at the end of the text.
3. Each chapter contains a concluding summary paragraph clearly stating the economic principles covered in the chapter.
4. Each chapter ends with discussion questions suitable for classroom use.

Through the years, many instructors have given us ideas, suggestions, and criticisms. For this edition, we were able to obtain the helpful written comments of the following reviewers: Eleanor Craig, University of Delaware; Bassam Harik, Western Michigan University; David Easley, Cornell University; Ashley Lyman, University of Idaho; and James McLain, University of New Orleans. To these reviewers, we wish to express our sincere appreciation for their numerous helpful comments. We also wish to thank the many other instructors who have written us. Additionally, we would like to thank Lavina Leed Miller for her helpful editorial assistance in preparing this edition. Shawn G. Miller was responsible for the revision of Chapter 16, The Economics of Professional Sports. As always, we take responsiblity for any remaining errors. We continue to welcome all comments and suggestions for change.

Douglass C. North
Roger LeRoy Miller

part one
Supply and Demand

INTRODUCTION

Supply and demand analysis forms the basis of virtually all economic analysis. In this part, we look at a number of issues, some of which do not appear to lend themselves to economic analysis. Nonetheless, each and every issue does, in fact, have an economic aspect. As you read about illicit drugs, agricultural products, **minimum wages**, and water, for example, you will find that supply and demand analysis applies throughout.

While reading about these issues, keep in mind the following:

1. The **law of demand** and the **law of supply** are given, holding other things constant.
2. A change in price affects quantities demanded and supplied. A change in any other nonprice variable shifts the entire demand or supply curve; in other words, there is a clear distinction between quantity demanded and supplied and demand and supply.
3. The laws of supply and demand relate price per **constant quality unit** to quantities supplied and demanded.

It is not necessary for everyone to react to price changes for the laws of demand and supply to be valid; the only requirement is that *some* marginal buyers or marginal producers react to price changes. In economics, all movement is on the margin.

1

the economics of
Euphoria

Marijuana is normally illegal; so are cocaine, methamphetamine, hashish, mescaline, dimethyltriptamine, psilocybin, and tetrahydrocannabinol. The illegality of these drugs does not, of course, prevent their use by young and old alike. It does, however, add certain peculiar characteristics to their production, distribution, and usage.

Before we look at drugs, we can learn a few things by examining a historical experience that proved unforgettable to most who lived through it—Prohibition.

On January 16, 1920, the Eighteenth Amendment to the United States Constitution became effective. It prohibited the "manufacture, sale, or transportation of intoxicating liquors within, or the import into, or export from the United States for beverage purposes." The Volstead Act, passed in 1919 to reinforce the Eighteenth Amendment, forbade the purchase, possession, and use of intoxicating liquors.[1]

A once-legal commodity became illegal overnight. The results were impressive, but they certainly could have been predicted by any economist. Since the legal supply of liquor and wine fell to practically zero and much of the public continued to demand the commodity, substitutes were quickly provided. Supplies of illegal liquor and wine flowed into the market. Increasing quantities of whiskey clandestinely found their way across the border from Canada, where its production was legal.

Of course, fewer entrepreneurs were now willing to provide the U.S. public with liquor. Why? Mainly because the cost of doing business suddenly increased. Potential speakeasy operators had to take into account a high risk of being jailed and/or fined. They also faced increased costs in operating a bar, for the usual business matters had to be carried on in a surreptitious (i.e., more costly) way. Moreover, speakeasy operators had to face the inevitable: an encounter with organized crime. They could look forward to paying off organized crime in addition to the local cops. Payments to the former reduced the possibility of cement shoes and the East River. Payments to the latter reduced the probability of landing in jail.

As a general summation, it could be said that Prohibition probably decreased the amount of alcoholic beverages that entrepreneurs were willing to provide *at the same prices as before*. If a bottle of one's favorite Scotch was available for $3 in 1919, either it would have cost more in 1920 or it would have been filled with a lower-quality product.

Whiskey lovers faced another problem during Prohi-

[1]Wine intended for religious purposes was excepted. A report of the Federal Council of the Churches of Christ in America showed that nearly 3 million gallons of sacramental wine were withdrawn in 1924 from government warehouses. This leads to interesting speculation about whether Prohibition somehow made Americans suddenly more religious.

bition. They could no longer read the newspaper ads and billboards to find the best buys in bourbon. Information had gone underground, and even knowledge about quality and price had suddenly become a much dearer commodity. In general, consumers have several means of obtaining information. They can find out about products from friends, from advertisements, and from personal experience. When goods are legal, they can be trademarked for identification. The trademark cannot be copied, and the courts protect it. Given such easily identified brands, consumers can be made aware of the quality and price of each via the recommendations of friends and ads. If their experience with a product does not jibe with their anticipations, they can assure themselves of no further encounter with the "bad" product by never buying that brand again.

When a general class of products becomes illegal, there are fewer ways of obtaining information on product quality. Brand names are no longer protected by the law, so falsification of well-known ones ensues. It becomes difficult to determine which trademarks are the "best." We therefore can understand why some unfortunate imbibers were blinded or killed by the effects of bad whiskey. The risk of something far more serious than a hangover become very real.

For some, the new whiskey-drinking costs were outweighed by the illicit joys of the speakeasy atmosphere. But other drinkers with more sensitive ethics were repelled by liquor's illegality and were deterred from consuming as much as they had before Prohibition, even if the liquor were obtainable at the same price as before.

While it is difficult to assess the net effect of these considerations, one fact is clear. Prohibition differed in its impact on the rich and the poor.

High-income drinkers were not particularly put out at having to pay more for the kind of whiskey they wanted. They ran little risk of being blinded, because neither the high price tag nor the cost of obtaining information about quality and supply could separate them from their favorite beverage. Presumably they would have been quite willing, before Prohibition, to pay more than the going price.

On the contrary, some lower-income imbibers had probably been paying just about their top limit for whiskey of acceptable quality before Prohibition. The sudden rise in price left them two alternatives: do without or settle for less, in the form of bootleg booze and bathtub gin. The distribution of injury, sickness, and death due to drinking contaminated whiskey directly mirrored the **distribution of income**.

There is an obvious analogy between what happened during Prohibition (the "noble experiment") and what is now happening with respect to most euphorics and hallucinogens. Like bootleg liquor, these drugs share the stricture of illegality which leads to both relatively high costs and high risk in their manufacture, distribution, sale, and consumption.[2] Yet there is a difference between the two periods in the matter of who obtains the more-wanted product. The wealthy user still is able to buy quality; he or she may even pay intermediaries to do the necessary shopping around. But while the middle-income user ends up getting inferior drugs, it seems likely that the "regular users," who are almost always poor, often get hold of the better-quality euphorics, and often at prices below those paid by others. The reason for this situation involves a mixture of economics and sociology. First, these users are poor because they are working at low-paying jobs—if they are working at all. Therefore, when they spend time away from their jobs, not much is lost. Thus, we say that the **opportunity cost** of their not working is low compared to the opportunity cost of those with higher-paying jobs who must sacrifice more earnings when they choose not to work. The "poor" user merely responds to the low opportunity cost when he or she spends

[2]Although a number of states have in many ways "decriminalized" the use and possession of small quantities of marijuana.

more time seeking out the best buys in the urgently wanted drugs. This was true during Prohibition also, but it didn't have as much import because there did not exist such a large sociological class of regular users devoted to the whiskey "cult."

On the other hand, the problems that face a middle-income drug user are manifold. If this user spends time seeking out information about which euphorics to buy and where to find them, he or she is confronted with higher opportunity costs from time spent away from work. Potential jailing is a greater deterrent in terms of both opportunity costs and psychic and emotional costs. And since this individual is probably unable or unwilling to pay some intermediary to do the necessary searching (as the rich user would do), he or she will end up with drugs whose quality would be scorned by many low-income users.

Since the use of certain drugs is legal in other countries, why don't rich users fly overseas to obtain and use their drugs? Take the case of Nepal, where high-quality marijuana can be purchased for about 2 cents an ounce, while the price in the United States may run as high as $40 for the same quality and quantity. The relative price of the Nepalese euphoric is thus 1/2000 that of the U.S. euphoric. Or is it? When we consider the *total* cost, we see that we must include round-trip air fare to Nepal, plus the opportunity cost of the flight time (minus any monetary value placed on seeing that exotic country). The relative price of one ounce of legal Nepalese marijuana now becomes more like $\dfrac{\$.02 + \$800}{\$40} = 20$ times the U.S. price for illegal marijuana.[3]

Up to now we've been dealing mainly with the demand

[3]The added cost to the user of detection, conviction, and jail are, of course, not included in the $40 price for the U.S. euphoric. However, the probability of detection and the costs of conviction are sufficiently low in the United States so as not to induce anyone to pay 20 times more for the pleasure of smoking marijuana in Nepal without fear of arrest.

side of the illegal drug picture. We have looked at the determinants of how much people buy and how much they are willing to pay for a certain quality of euphorics. Now let's look briefly at the supply side. We wish to find out what determines how much people are willing to furnish of a certain quality of euphoric at different prices. This is known as the law of supply. The parallels to be made with the supply of whiskey during Prohibition are numerous. The illegality of the manufacture and distribution of most drugs poses a large risk to suppliers. The risk is higher the greater (1) the probability of detection, (2) the probability of conviction, and (3) the potential jail sentence and/or fine. Costs of doing business include measures to assure secrecy and avoid detection, payoffs to organized crime (for certain drugs not easily manufactured, like heroin), and potential payoffs to the police.

What would happen if marijuana were legalized? Should we expect a state of euphoria?

On the supply side, entrepreneurs would be able to supply larger quantities at the same price as before because the costs of doing business would fall. There would be no risks involved, no need for payoffs to organized crime, and no high cost of maintaining secrecy in production and distribution. The price would eventually fall to a level just covering the lower costs of legal production and legal distribution. In fact, we could even get more *cannabis* supplied if we were to repeat what happened in the colonial period. Then the English parliament established a bounty to encourage American planters to produce hemp, or *cannabis sativa*, the plant from which marijuana is produced. At that time *cannabis sativa* was a valuable article of American commerce. The seeds were used for oil, and the stalks of the plant could be fashioned into webbing, twine, bagging, and rope. The hemp fibers added durability to any material with which it was interwoven. The crop was important enough for King James I of England to declare it illegal for any settler who had hemp seeds not to plant them!

When there is unrestrained **competition** among the sellers of a legal product, it is difficult for relatively inferior products to exist side by side with better ones unless the price of the former is lower. Otherwise sellers of the superior product will inform the buying public of the anomaly. Since the product is legal, the free flow of information will assure that some buyers will refuse to purchase inferior products unless their price is correspondingly lower.

By opening the door to advertising, legalization would also reduce the costs of disseminating and obtaining information about supplies. Competition among sellers and increased information available to buyers would combine to raise the quality of the product.

On the demand side, legalization would, of course, eliminate the threats of detection, conviction, and jail, with their attendant costs. Because of higher overall quality, the risk of bad side effects from improperly prepared drugs would be lessened. Both of these cost reductions would lead consumers to demand a larger quantity even at the prices that had prevailed before legalization.

It is difficult to predict whether the price of marijuana would rise or fall immediately after legalization. Since consumers presumably would demand more, suppliers would produce more. If the increase in demand were to exceed that in supply, a shortage would result and consumers would find themselves paying high prices to obtain as much of the now-legal product as they wanted. In the long run, however, it could safely be predicted that prices would, as usual, fall to a level just covering the costs of production, distribution, and normal profit—which would certainly be lower than the price paid today. (In fact, given worldwide availability, we can safely assume that the supply of drugs in the United States is highly elastic at the approximate cost of production.)

If euphoric drugs in general were to be legalized and this chain of events occurred, one more link in the sequence would be a fall in the price of euphorics relative to that of alcoholic beverages. Would this lead to a trend away from drinking—and toward the smoking of marijuana, for example? The answer hinges on an "if." If marijuana is a *substitute* for alcohol, this might well happen. But if the two are **complementary** instead of substitutable, then increased use of marijuana would lead to increased use of alcohol.

In any event, the above analysis does not constitute an argument for or against legalization of euphorics. There are costs to society involved in each course. There are also benefits. Describing the costs of making something illegal does not necessarily argue for a change in the law. After all, there are costs involved in passing a law that forbids wife abandonment, but society obviously has decided that the benefits of making abandonment illegal far outweigh those costs.

SUMMARY

When a good or activity becomes illegal, there is typically a supply response and a demand response. Since illegality causes the cost of production to rise, the supply (curve) of an illegal good or activity will decrease. (The supply curve will shift inward to the left.) That means that a smaller quantity of the illegal good will be supplied at each and every price. On the demand side, we can predict that there will be some decrease in demand. (The demand curve will also shift inward to the left.) Historically, in such cases the supply decrease has been greater than the demand decrease, so the **market-clearing price** of the illegal good is greater than the market-clearing price of the legal good.

DISCUSSION QUESTIONS

1. Does supply and demand analysis apply equally well to so-called hard, or addictive, drugs, such as heroin?

2. What effect does the inability to advertise have on the variability of price per constant quality unit of an illegal good?

2

the economics of
Prostitution

In 1945, a French politician—one Mme. Marthe Richards—demanded closure of all Paris brothels. She claimed that the 178 licensed houses, 600 prostitute-serving hotels, 10,000 pimps, and 6000 ladies of the night were "undermining Parisian morals and health." Moreover, she estimated that the closing of brothels would make available 6000 rooms for students and those bombed out of their homes during the war.

The Municipal Council of Paris, impressed by her statistics, gave the brothels three months to shut down. The effects have been far-reaching, to say the least, and apparently have not proved too satisfactory, because recently a vigorous campaign has been shaping up in France to restore the legality of the world's oldest profession. Although the product differs considerably, the economic analysis of prostitution is similar to that of euphoria, with, of course, a few special twists.

The service that prostitutes offer for sale has, like all others, two dimensions: quantity and quality. In some sense, these two are interrelated; quantity can be increased by lowering quality. The quality of the service is, among other things, a function of (1) experience (*human capital investment*);[1] (2) the innate characteristics of the provider of the service, such as looks and intelligence; and (3) current operating expenditures, such as how much money is spent on appearance, surroundings, and health.

To be sure, *substitution* is possible among these three aspects of quality. Perhaps the same quality can be achieved either by being born beautiful or by spending effort and money on makeup and clothes. Some ladies of the night are able to compensate for poor looks by dressing well. In economic terms, they are able to substitute clothes for natural endowments.

For many who utilize the services of a prostitute, the health aspect of quality is of utmost importance. The decision to make prostitution illegal in France had notable consequences on the probability of some clients contracting venereal disease. Let's see why.

When prostitution was legal, numerous business establishments existed whose purpose in life was offering prostitutes' services. Since all was on the up-and-up, they could advertise without risk. Because clients could easily compare prices and qualities, information was relatively cheap. If it became common knowledge that the employees of one house spread venereal disease to their customers, that firm would either have to lower its prices drastically or suffer a drop in clientele.

Even though cheap information made it inadvisable for any firm to allow unhealthy employees to work (because

---

[1] You are making an investment in your own human capital by attending college and by reading this book.

clients would go elsewhere), the French government made doubly sure that venereal disease was kept at a minimum by requiring weekly medical inspections. Since most prostitutes worked in establishments, it was relatively easy to check all of them, and social disease was rare among prostitutes before 1947. The reader can easily draw the analogy between legalized prostitution and legalized narcotic usage.

When prostitution was legal, suppliers of the service charged their opportunity cost, with no "risk" factor added, since no threat of imprisonment or fines existed. Those demanding the service had no need to invest large amounts of their resources (time and effort) obtaining information that would help them avoid the risk of a poor-quality product, as represented by the threat of venereal disease.

What has happened in France since 1947? Obviously there are no more legal houses of prostitution. The prostitutes, for the most part, have taken to the streets. The cost of doing business has increased. Streetwalkers must avoid detection and arrest either by cleverness or by paying off police. Some must stay outside more than before, adding a cost of discomfort. Also, they no longer benefit from the **economies of scale** that previously kept down the cost of such "accessories" to their trade as an attractive atmosphere. At the same wages as before, then, fewer prostitutes were willing to stay in the profession after 1947. (Thus, the **supply schedule** shifted inward to the left.)

On the demand side, clients could no longer be so confident about the quality of the product, because competition among legal houses was removed. Previously, any house that got a bad reputation suffered. But now individual prostitutes can more easily lower quality (i.e., have a venereal disease) and still obtain clients, for information has become much more difficult to obtain. And, of course, there are no longer government medical inspections. Such a situation would be roughly equivalent to a system of Food and Drug Administration (FDA) inspection and labeling of different grades of marijuana in our own country.

Predictably, as information about quality has become more expensive, the wealthy citizen has been the one able to pay the cost of seeking out the healthy prostitutes, while the poor have contracted venereal disease. But the cost of illegal prostitution affects others in the society. If a middle-class marijuana user dies from some arsenic in an illegal cigarette, the rest of society bears little of the cost. But if a dock worker contracts a venereal disease, he is not alone in bearing the cost, because he can spread the disease to others. This explains in part why there is currently so much fervor in France about legalizing prostitution again: The rates of venereal disease have soared among those associated with the prostitution industry, suppliers and demanders alike.

SUMMARY

The prohibiting of prostitution in France caused a decrease in the number (or growth rate) and in the average quality of prostitutes, probably a decrease in the number of demanders (even at the same prices as before), and probably a rise in the average price to the customer. As an added effect, venereal disease became more common among common folk.

DISCUSSION QUESTIONS

1. What similarities are there between the economic analysis of prostitution and the economic analysis of illegal euphoric drugs?
2. Predict the results of legalization of prostitution throughout the United States. What if prostitution were legalized only in major cities?

3

the economics of
Staying Alive
at 55 MPH

Temporary shortages in the supply of a product can sometimes, through a ripple effect throughout the economy, lead
to surprisingly permanent results. Back in the depressing
days of the oil shortage in 1973 and 1974, for example, a
reduction of the maximum speed limit on interstate highways from 70 to 55 MPH was mandated for every state in
the nation. It was argued that at speeds higher than 55 MPH,
fuel consumption increased dramatically; in order to conserve precious energy, the speed limit was lowered.

Few disputed the economic good sense of the speed-
limit reduction under those circumstances. Now that oil
"shortages" no longer exist, however, many argue that the
speed limit should be raised, particularly in the western
states. Westerners argue that the 55-MPH limit is unreason-
able for the distances they drive and that billions of hours

in driving time are wasted each year as a result of the "temporary" 1974 speed limit.

The argument for keeping the 55-MPH speed limit has centered on the assumption that the lower speed limit has reduced accidents and highway fatalities. According to the U.S. Department of Transportation (DOT), the lower speed limit has saved many thousands of lives per year. There are several issues that must be examined when analyzing this argument. One has to do with the cost to society—in terms of "wasted travel time"—per life saved, and the other has to do with whether, in fact, it was the lower speed limit that was responsible for saving those many thousands of lives per year or some other economic factor.

One economist, Charles A. Lave, undertook a study to estimate the cost per life saved by looking at the opportunity cost of driving 55 miles an hour compared to 65 miles an hour. That is, he looked at the additional time that commuters had to spend at the lower speed limit and then placed a value on this additional time. He valued each hour of extra time at 42 percent of the commuters' hourly wages. The result was startling. In 1978, the 55-MPH speed limit cost Americans about $6 billion in travel time per year. The government estimated that the lower speed limit had saved 4500 lives that year. If we divide $6 billion by 4500 lives, then each life saved cost $1.3 million. Compare this cost with some other life-saving activities: A smoke detector put in every home would cost about $5,000 per life saved; a mobile cardiac care unit costs about $2,000 per life saved; kidney dialysis machines can save lives for $30,000; finally, highway improvements cost approximately $50,000 per life saved.

To put it another way, Lave pointed out that the cost of saving one life by dropping the speed limit from 65 MPH to 55 MPH is over 100 person-years of extra travel time per year!

What about the DOT's contention that highway deaths have been cut by the lower speed limit? A small but growing band of researchers claims that the evidence is to the contrary. First of all, the highway fatality rate has actually been trending downward since the days of the horseless carriage. In 1922, for example, 18 people died for every 100 million miles traveled. By 1945, only 10 people died for every 100 million miles traveled. Fatality rates have fallen, on average, slightly over 3 percent a year since then. In support of its argument for the lower speed limit, the DOT points to the fact that in 1974, the year the lower limit was put into effect, fatality rates dropped over 15 percent to 3.6 fatalities per 100 million miles traveled. This was the sharpest one-year drop in traffic history and, according to the DOT, the result of the lower speed limit. But, strangely enough, over the next 10 years the fatality rate dropped more than 25 percent. Much of this decrease occurred in just one year—1982—when the fatality rate dropped 12.7 percent. What had happened during this 10-year period, and particularly in 1982, to cause this reduction? Certainly not a further decrease in the speed limit. In fact, more and more people were ignoring the maximum speed limit, and by 1982 the average speed on interstate highways was almost 68 MPH.

According to some researchers, the reduction in traffic deaths has less to do with the speed limit than with other economic factors affecting transportation. It has been shown, for example, that recreational drivers tend to have more accidents because they travel on unfamiliar roads and are often tired. In 1974, when the number of traffic fatalities was sharply reduced, there had also been a notable cutback in recreational driving because of the gas shortage. In 1982, again a year when the number of traffic deaths dropped precipitously, recreational driving also was less than usual because of the **recession** of that year. Further, in a 1983 study (produced by the DOT!) it was shown that 98 percent of the variation in annual highway fatalities could be accounted for by changes in economic factors, such as the unemployment rate.

The argument continues. Researchers such as Lave contend that accidents are not caused by speed, but by variations in the speed of cars on the highway at the same time. He argues that highway patrol officers should pay as much or more attention to slow drivers as they do to fast ones. In any event, a number of states have been quite lax in enforcing their speed limits, particularly in the western states where there are long stretches of interstate highway between cities and little traffic congestion. If the present pressure on Congress continues by the lawmakers from the western states, we may well see a change in the maximum speed limit to 65 MPH in the not-too-distant future. In the meantime, individual states are reluctant to act on their own. In 1986, for example, the Nevada state legislature voted to raise its interstate speed limit to 70 MPH. The bill was vetoed by the governor. Why? Because the federal government would have eliminated $130 million in federal funds to that state. State governments know about opportunity costs, too.

SUMMARY

Because of a decrease in the supply of oil brought on by the oil shortage of 1973, the U.S. government instituted a series of measures to reduce oil and gasoline consumption. Perhaps the most long-lasting of these "temporary" measures was the imposition of the 55-MPH speed limit on all interstate highways throughout the nation. Many people, particularly from the western states, have wanted to raise the speed limit back to 70 MPH, or at least 65 MPH, now that the oil crisis is over. The government maintained for many years that the lower speed limit resulted in many lives being saved and should be retained for this reason. Critics pointed out that the opportunity cost—in terms of "wasted travel time"—per life saved by driving at the lower speed has been disproportionately high relative to the cost of other life-saving devices and safety improvements. Further, research indicates that factors other than the lower speed limit should be credited for the reduction in traffic fatalities in recent years.

DISCUSSION QUESTIONS

1. What other factors not mentioned in the above issue might account for the reduction in traffic fatalities in the United States in the past 10 years?
2. Do you think the opportunity cost of saving one life can ever be "too high"?

4

the economics of
Raising Less Corn and More Hell

When Mary Lease stumped the Kansas countryside in 1890, she urged the farmers to raise "less corn and more hell," and that's just what they began to do.

In the late nineteenth century, their activities took the form of political campaigns aimed toward (1) expanding the **money supply**, which they felt would increase agricultural prices faster than other prices; (2) introducing railroad rate regulation designed to lower freight rates for transporting agricultural products; and (3) curbing monopolies, which they felt would reduce their costs for commodities. When prices of farm goods rose at the start of the twentieth century, the farmers stuck to raising their corn, and during World War I they expanded their production dramatically in response to soaring prices. Then after the war European countries imposed high taxes on any agricultural goods crossing their borders. Along with other factors, this restriction reduced the amount of corn that American farmers could sell. Farm prices fell sharply in the 1920s and farm organizations began to view their problem as one of relative overproduction. Numerous cooperative efforts were made to restrict production, but these efforts failed (except in the case of a few specialty crops such as tobacco, where the relatively small number of producers made mutual agreement more feasible). Most crops were produced under competitive conditions, that is, a large number of sellers (and buyers) dealt in a product that was undifferentiated (one farmer's corn was just the same as another farmer's corn). Accordingly, it was impossible for producers to organize themselves on a voluntary basis. But what farmers failed to do by voluntary cooperation in the 1920s, they accomplished via governmental directives in the 1930s. A farm **price-support** program was instituted then that marked the beginning of a policy of farm subsidization in this country that has continued until the present time.

We can best understand the results of price supports by first examining the market for agricultural commodities prior to price supports. In that competitive market, a large number of farmers supplied a commodity—we'll use peanuts as our example. The sum of the quantities that individual farmers will supply at various prices makes up the **aggregate supply** schedule of a commodity. Each farmer supplies only a small part of the aggregate. He cannot influence the price of the product. If he raised his price, anyone wishing to purchase peanuts could easily buy from someone else at the **market-clearing**, or **equilibrium**, **price.** And no farmer would sell below the market-clearing price because he would make less money than possible, since he can sell all that he produces at the market-clearing price. Thus, every unit of output sold by farmers goes for the same price. The price received for the last (*marginal*) unit sold is exactly the same as that received for all the rest.

The farmer will produce peanuts up to the point at

which if one more unit were produced, its production cost would be greater than the price received. Every farmer faces the same production decision. Notice that at higher prices, farmers can incur higher costs for additional units produced and still make a **profit**, so at higher prices, all farmers together will produce more. But, again, no farmer alone can influence the price. No farmer will stop producing until he stops making a profit. That is, each farmer will end up selling peanuts at the market-clearing price, which will equal his costs of production plus a *normal profit*.[1]

The price at which each farmer can sell his peanuts depends on how people feel about buying them, and that depends on their preferences, incomes, and the prices of substitutes. The demand for food in general is quite unresponsive to price changes because there are no close substitutes for food. The demand for peanuts is more responsive to price changes because of available substitutes. Even so, it takes a drastic reduction in the price of peanuts to get people to buy a lot more. Conversely, an increase in unit price doesn't cause people to buy much less, since there is relatively little **price elasticity of demand** for peanuts. This situation has implications for peanut farmers.

Agricultural costs of production and output can vary greatly from year to year because of, among other things, variations in weather. During a good year, production may be relatively large. But since the demand for peanuts is relatively inelastic, farmers will have to reduce drastically the price of their peanut crop if they are to sell it all. They may even have to sustain a loss that year. The opposite situation occurs when production is small one year because of, say, a drought.

In sum, the short-run competitive market in peanuts results in changing prices of the product and changing profits for the producers.

---

[1]This is actually a cost to society, since it is required to keep him farming peanuts instead of changing to an alternative occupation.

Now how has the usual price-support program worked? The government decided what constituted a "fair price." The formula for this vital determination was the ratio between the prices farmers historically paid for what they bought and the prices they received for their crops in "good" years. How could the government make this arbitrary price "stick" since it was above the level that would have prevailed otherwise?[2] It agreed to buy the peanuts at that (**parity**) price.[3] Actually, the purchase was disguised as a loan from the **Commodity Credit Corporation** (CCC) that never needed to be repaid. Historically, the government has either stored the peanuts or sold them on the world market (as opposed to the domestic market) at the going price. Since World War II, the world price has often been well below the support price; thus, the government has taken a "loss." For example, in 1976, the support price for nonedible "crushing" peanuts (used for their oil) was $394 per ton, but the world market price was $256 per ton. In effect, then, the U.S. government has been providing **subsidies** to peanut farmers to the tune of $50 to $200 million per year.

In order to prevent too great a **surplus**, the government in 1941 allowed a maximum of 1.6 million acres to be used for peanut production. However, the yield per acre has tripled since then and the allotments haven't been cut back. Moreover, a large quantity of "illegal" peanuts—peanuts grown on land not officially allowed by the original allotment program—has been grown in the past few years. Since there has been as much as $165 per ton gross profit to be made by selling the peanuts at the support price, it is not surprising that some farmers have wanted to grow peanuts "illegally."

Price supports mean two things, then: (1) higher prices to the consumer for those products whose fixed (parity) price

[2]Called the market equilibrium price.
[3]This is one possibility only; usually the support price has been between 75 and 90 percent of parity.

exceeds the price that would otherwise prevail, and (2) more governmental resources (taxpayers' money) expended in agriculture than would otherwise be spent.[4]

By and large, since the 1930s our agricultural economy has been affected by a patchwork policy on the part of the government consisting of price supports and—when surpluses mount—of incentives to restrict acreage under cultivation. We are now paying the price for such a policy in the form of the current agricultural crisis, which shows no signs of being alleviated in the near future. Why? As you might suspect, the answer has something to do with supply and demand.

In a sense, under the price-support system American farmers have been "too successful"—to the point where supply has dramatically outstripped demand for agricultural products. Surpluses of farm products have become typical over the past decade, and the government dole of free milk and cheese has become a routine part of American life. The government stockpiles of agricultural surpluses have grown enormously in the past few years, and by 1986, according to one observer, the CCC had enough wheat in its storage bins to make seven loaves of bread for every man, woman, and child in the world. There are currently 5 billion surplus bushels of corn in CCC granaries and mountains of soybeans, beet sugar, and other farm products in storage bins or caves owned or rented by the CCC.

By the Farm Security Act of 1985 the Reagan administration hoped to alleviate the problem of overproduction and surpluses—and increase farmers' income—by encouraging exports. This meant, however, lowering support prices for agricultural commodities to a level where they could be competitive on world markets. In order to compensate for the lower support prices, "target prices" for agricultural

[4]Additionally, resources were and are devoted to getting and keeping those subsidy payments; the illegal milk co-op payments exposed during the Watergate investigations are a case in point.

products were established. If the market price fell below the target price for, say, wheat, then the government would pay the difference. Ideally, this shift in government policy—toward letting world markets set domestic agricultural prices—would eventually wean American farmers from dependence on the government for support and subsidies.

In the year since its inception, however, the policy had little success; surpluses continued to grow, and thousands of farmers were quitting the business or losing their farms to their mortgage-holders as net farm income continued to fall. By pinning its hopes on the export market, the government overlooked the fact that the world market for agricultural commodities has changed considerably in the past decade, and U.S. exports of food are no longer needed by former markets. India and China, for example, are now self-sufficient in foods. Saudi Arabia now has surpluses of its own—stored in idle oil tankers—to worry about. Brazil, after nearly doubling its land under cultivation in the last decade, has now become a net exporter of agricultural products. The "green revolution" in the Third World—made possible, ironically, by U.S. foreign aid—has helped to transform the global market for food products. As a result of the changing world food market, U.S. exports of agricultural products are declining instead of increasing, and for the first time since 1971 this country saw a negative trade balance for these products in 1986.

Instead of being eased off of price supports and subsidies, farmers remain as dependent as ever on the government for assistance. Estimates of the expenses of the new farm policy launched by the Farm Security Act ranged from $24 billion to $31 billion for 1986 alone. Given the problem of the federal **deficit** and the need to cut government expenses, the future for the farming sector is not too bright. For 50 years, farmers have been conditioned to come to the public trough for support. Now the question is: What happens when that trough runs dry?

SUMMARY

An unrestricted market for farm products yields an equilib-rium price at which the quantity demanded equals the quan-tity supplied. A price support system will lead to an excess quantity supplied if the price support price is above the mar-ket-clearing price and if there is some means by which the "surplus" is taken care of. Typically, the government has purchased, in one way or another, "surplus" farm products. Surpluses are currently mounting in government storage bins because increased global agricultural productivity has reduced, or eliminated entirely, their need for U.S. food products. The lesson to be learned from the history of the agricultural sector is that both consumers and producers re-spond to disequilibrium situations: Relatively high prices, whether caused by market forces or government interven-tion, motivate producers to produce more and consumers to consume less.

DISCUSSION QUESTIONS

1. How could price supports create a shortage of, for example, corn in one year and surpluses in another?
2. Overall, do you think American farmers have been helped or harmed by price supports?

5

the economics of
Minimum Wages

In an unrestricted labor market, there will be an equilibrium wage rate at which the quantity of labor demanded will equal the quantity supplied. In essence, any analysis of labor markets is equivalent to the supply-demand analysis for any product sold. The analysis of minimum wage legislation is similar to the analysis of any restriction on the market price for a particular product. If we look at employment in different industries and among different groups of individuals, we find that certain industries and some specific groups in the labor force seem consistently to experience unusually high rates of unemployment. For example, teenagers—black teenagers in particular—have for many years now experienced rates of unemployment two and three times those of other subgroups in the labor force. To understand why different groups experience differential rates of unemployment,

we must look at the history and effect of minimum wage
legistation.

At the turn of the century, minimum wage legislation
grew out of the general movement against the "exploitation
of the poor working girl" and the low pay for workers toiling
in what were then considered bad working conditions, or
"sweatshops." By 1913, seven states had imposed compul-
sory minimum wage rates applicable to women and minors.
During President Roosevelt's New Deal, a federal minimum
wage was set as part of the National Industrial Recovery Act
(NIRA). However, the NIRA was declared unconstitutional
by the Supreme Court in 1937 and so, too, were the minimum wages established under it. Within a year, though, the
Fair Labor Standards Act was passed, which established a
minimum wage of 25 cents for all industries involved in interstate commerce. This act has remained the basis for all
federal minimum wage legislation. Since that time, minimum wages have gradually increased to their current level.

To analyze the effects of any kind of minimum wage
legislation, we must first answer this question: What determines the wage rate that workers are paid in the absence of
restrictions? Basically, in the aggregate, employers will hire
workers up to the point where the value of the additional
output made possible by the new worker just equals the increase in the employer's wage bill. In other words, on the
margin, workers are paid what they are worth to the employer.[1] When a wage rate is arbitrarily increased, some marginal workers become unprofitable to employ. Given a constant **aggregate demand**, a higher wage rate imposed by a
government-legislated minimum wage means that some employers can no longer afford to employ those marginal workers because the market value of their contribution to total
output is less than the minimum wage.

Workers who lose their jobs, who are not rehired, or
who cannot find jobs at the minimum wage receive no wage

[1]The wage rate equals the **value of marginal product**.

at all. They must find jobs in sectors of the economy that are not covered by minimum wage legislation. But to induce employers in these other sectors to take on additional workers, wage rates in these sectors must, by necessity, fall. Hence, by eliminating marginal job opportunities in industries it covers, the minimum wage hurts some of the very people it was intended to help.

True, a change of a few cents in the minimum wage may not greatly affect the total employment picture. However, consider what happened in 1956 when the minimum wage jumped from 75 cents to $1 an hour, an increase of one-third. A few years later, the Secretary of Labor concluded in a report that "there were significant declines in employment in most of the low-wage industries studied."

Which group of workers constitutes "marginal" workers? Those with the least experience and the least amount of training and education—in other words, the teenage labor force. Teenagers generally have the lowest productivity in the economy. Indeed, it is by working on a low-paid job that teenagers can increase their productivity and hence their future income potential. The data bear out our prediction that they would be most affected by the minimum wage. In 1956, when there was a one-third jump in the minimum wage, nonwhite teenage unemployment increased from 13 percent to more than 24 percent! A 1965 study by Arthur Burns concluded that "the ratio of the unemployment rate of teenagers to that of male adults was invariably higher during the six months following an increase in the minimum wage than it was in the preceding half year."

Increases in the minimum wage have another effect that is perhaps less well known. They increase the demand[2] for other types of workers, that is, for substitute workers or, more specifically, higher-skilled, higher-paid union workers. We can assume that a certain amount of substitution is possible between union workers and nonunion workers, even

[2]The demand schedule shifts (outward) to the right.

though the latter are generally less skilled, particularly those among them who may be affected by minimum wage legislation. At a low enough price, an employer will find it profitable to hire more lower-skilled nonunion workers in the place of fewer high-skilled and higher-paid union workers. However, as the relative price of nonunion, lower-skilled workers rises, the employer finds it less advantageous to hire them in place of the more expensive union workers. It is not surprising, therefore, that the strongest supporters of increases in the minimum wage are unions and members of Congress representing states that are heavily unionized, particularly in the North.

The effects of a minimum wage law depend crucially upon whether or not it is enforced. If the law is not enforced, it may have no effect whatsoever. The analysis of minimum wages is identical to the analysis of price controls. Although it is easy to analyze the effects of minimum wage legislation, because the law spells out specifically which kinds of labor are covered and what exemptions are allowed, it does not always follow that the minimum wage is effective.

There are ways to circumvent minimum wage laws. In every instance where low-paid workers are receiving benefits in kind, such as below-cost lunches or free tickets to professional football games, there can be a substitution of increases in money wages for benefits in kind. For example, if a minimum wage forces money wages to go up, the employer can raise the price of lunches or charge for professional football tickets to make up the difference between the new minimum wage and the former lower-wage rate. Furthermore, firms may require kickbacks from employees, establish company stores, or require workers to live in company-owned housing. The new prices for company-store products or company-owned housing may now exceed their market value. This amounts to paying a lower wage. If a minimum wage is forced on the employer, the actual wage can still be kept below the legal minimum by use of these devices.

Another method to avoid the minimum wage loss is to

hire relatives. In many cases, relatives of employers, particularly close relatives, are not covered under minimum wage laws and/or are not monitored closely by the Department of Labor. This way of avoiding minimum wage laws may be a clue to understanding how small neighborhood grocery stores and restaurants can successfully compete with larger, presumably more efficient enterprises in their area. Dry-cleaning establishments owned by retired couples apparently are competing very effectively with the larger dry-cleaning chains, presumably because of the former's ability to avoid minimum wage legislation. (The owners of the firm don't have to pay themselves any particular wage rate.)

We also must be careful to distinguish between the short run and the long run. It is a general proposition that short-run curves tend to be less elastic than long-run curves. Hence, we would expect the minimum wage to have a much smaller effect in the short run than in the long run. What we need to know (in order to assess its full impact on employment) is what happens in the long run.

The most recent research on the effect of minimum wages indicates that minimum wage legislation weakens the economic status of those at the bottom of the distribution of earnings. The apparent redistribution of income that occurs as a result of the minimum wage appears to be from some "have nots" to other "have nots." Additionally, the most skilled low-wage workers are the very ones who are not put out of work by increases in the minimum wage rate. The poorest group—workers who are likely to be the least productive—are the most likely to become unemployed as a result of minimum wage rate increases.

To counter the effects of the minimum wage on teenagers, particularly black teenagers, and reduce the high rate of unemployment for this group of largely unskilled workers, a "subminimum wage" of $2.50 per hour has been proposed by President Reagan in recent years. The **subminimum wage** would allow employers to hire teenagers for temporary summer work at a price that corresponds more closely than the minimum wage to their skills (or lack of them). Supporters of the subminimum wage estimate that it would create 400,000 jobs, mostly for minority teenagers. As might be expected, the chief opposition to the subminimum wage has been organized labor, and so far the bill has not met with success in Congress.

SUMMARY

To the extent that minimum wage legislation is effectively enforced, it reduces employment possibilities for individuals whose productivity is such that the value of their marginal product is less than the legislated minimum wage. Minimum wage legislation therefore creates unemployment for the relatively untrained and unskilled—teenagers, members of minorities, the very old. To counter the effects of the minimum wage on teenagers, a "subminimum wage" of $2.50 an hour has been proposed by President Reagan. To date, however, largely because of opposition from organized labor, Congress has not passed the proposed legislation.

DISCUSSION QUESTIONS

1. What effect does inflation have on our minimum wage analysis?
2. What are some of the ways that employers can avoid paying minimum wages?
3. Despite the above arguments, make the best case you can in favor of minimum wage legislation.

the economics of
Water

Water threatens to become a major issue of the late 1980s and 1990s. Conservationists are increasingly concerned about the toxic contamination of our water supply and the depletion of our underground water sources. Extensive irrigation projects in the western states use approximately 150 billion gallons of water a day—seven times as much water as all the nation's city water systems combined. The Ogallala aquifer (a 20-million-acre lake beneath the beef and bread basket states of Colorado, Kansas, Nebraska, New Mexico, Oklahoma, and Texas) is currently dropping by three feet a year. Why? Because of the 150,000 wells pumping water out faster than nature can replenish it.

The common view of water is that it is a precious **resource** that is being overused and yes, indeed, we are running out of it. The economic analysis of the water problem, however, is not quite so pessimistic nor so tied to the physical quantities of water that exist on our earth and in the atmosphere. Rather, an economic analysis of water follows along lines similar to an analysis of any other **scarce** resource.

The water industry is one of the oldest and largest in the United States. The philosophy surrounding the water industry merits some analysis. Many commentators believe that water is unique, that is should not be treated as an **economic good**, that is, a scarce good. Engineering studies that concern themselves with demand for residential water typically use a "requirements" approach. The forecaster simply predicts population changes and then multiplies those estimates by the currently available data showing the average amount of water used per person. The underlying assumption for such a forecast is that regardless of the price charged for water in the future, the same quantity will be demanded. Implicitly, then, both the short- and long-run price elasticities of demand are assumed to be zero.

But is this really the case? Perhaps not. Consider, for example, the cities of Tucson and Phoenix, Arizona. Although these cities are located only 100 miles apart, their water-usage rates are notably different. While the average household in Phoenix uses 260 gallons per day, in Tucson the average usage is only 160 gallons per day. Could this usage differential be accounted for by the fact that water costs $13.76 per 2350 cubic feet in Phoenix, while Tucson users pay $24.27 for the same amount of water? Before we jump to such a conclusion, let's look at a study of water prices in Boulder, Colorado, conducted by economist Steve Hanke.

Boulder was selected by Hanke because in 1961 the water utility in Boulder installed water meters in every home and business that it supplied. Prior to 1961, Boulder, like many other municipalities in the United States, had charged a flat monthly rate for water. Each household paid a specified amount of dollars per month no matter how much (or little) water was used. In essence, the flat fee charged prior to 1961 meant that a zero price was being charged at the margin (for any incremental use of water). The introduction of usage meters meant that a positive price for the marginal unit of water was now imposed.

Hanke looked at the quantity of water demanded both before and after the meters were installed in Boulder.[1] Hanke first developed what he calls the "ideal" use of water for each month throughout the year. He completed his "ideal" use estimates by taking account of the average irrigable area per residence, the average temperature during the month, the average number of daylight hours, and the effect of rainfall. The term *ideal* implies nothing from an economic point of view, merely indicating the minimum quantity of sprinkling water required to maintain the aesthetic quality of each residence's lawn.

From the data in Table 6-1, which compares water usage in Boulder with and without metering, we find that individuals sprinkled their lawns much more under the flat-rate system than they did under the metered-rate system. The data presented in column 3 of the table are for the one-year period after the metering system was put into effect.

Column 1 shows the meter route numbers arbitrarily assigned by the municipality. Column 2 shows how much water was used in the different routes during the period when a flat rate was charged for water usage. It is expressed in terms of actual sprinkling compared to "ideal" sprinkling. In column 3, actual sprinkling is compared to "ideal" sprinkling, but under a system of metered-rate pricing in which each user is charged for the actual amount of water used. Hanke's data indicate that the quantity of water demanded is a function of the price charged for water. Moreover, Hanke found that for many years after the imposition of the metered-rate pricing system for water, the quantity of water de-

[1]"Demand for Water under Dynamic Conditions," *Water Resources Research*, vol. 6, no. 5 (October 1970), pp. 1253–1261.

TABLE 6-1 Comparing Water Usage with and without Metering of Actual Usage

(1) Meter Routes	(2) Actual Sprinkling to Ideal Sprinkling, Flat Rate Period	(3) Actual Sprinkling to Ideal Sprinkling, Metered Rate Period
16, 18	128	78
37	175	72
53, 54	156	72
70, 71, 72	177	63
73, 75	175	97
74	175	102
76, 78	176	105
79	157	86

Source: Steve Hanke, "Demand for Water under Dynamic Conditions," *Water Resources Research*, vol. 6, no. 5 (October 1970).

manded not only remained at a lower level than before metering, but continued to fall slightly. That, of course, means that the long-run price elasticity of demand for water was greater than the short-run price elasticity of demand.

Would attaching a dollar sign to water help to solve problems of recurring water **shortages** and endemic waste? Some economists feel it would. It is well known, for example, that much of the water supplied by federal irrigation projects is wasted by farmers and other users because they have no incentive to conserve water and curb overconsumption. The federal government, which has subsidized water projects since 1902, allots water to certain districts, communities, or farmers on the basis of previous usage "requirements." That means that if farmers in a certain irrigation district were to conserve on water usage by, say, upgrading their irrigation systems, their water allotment would eventually be reduced. As a result, a "use it or lose it" attitude has prevailed among users of federal water. Water supplied by federal water projects is also cheap. The Congressional

Budget Office has estimated that users pay only about 19 percent of the total cost of the water they get.

Economists have suggested that raising the price of federal water would lead to more efficient and less wasteful water consumption. A study by B. Delworth Gardner, an economist at the University of California at Davis, for example, concludes that a 10 percent rise in prices could reduce water use on some California farm crops by as much as 20 percent. Support for such a price rise is politically difficult, however, because federal law stipulates that ability to pay, as well as cost, must be considered when determining water payments.

An alternative solution has been proposed by some economists, involving the trading and sale of water rights held by existing federal water users. Such a solution, it is felt, would benefit the economy overall because it could help curb water waste, prevent water shortages, and lessen the need for costly new water projects. To some extent, trading and sales of water rights have already taken place, for example in California and Utah. But numerous federal and state laws have, to date, made such trading very difficult.

Until recent years, it had been thought that there was so much water we simply did not have to worry about it— there was always another river or another well to draw on if we ran short. Putting a price tag on water would require a substantial change in the way we have traditionally thought about water. Is this possible or even desirable? This is the basic question facing Americans today.

SUMMARY

Conservationists and others are increasingly concerned about the toxic contamination and depletion of our water resources. Extensive irrigation projects in the western states use vast quantities of water—more than can be replenished by nature. An economist will argue that water shortages and waste exist because of an improper pricing system in which individuals are not forced to pay the full social opportunity cost of the water used. There is increasing evidence that at a higher price for water the demand can be decreased substantially. To prevent further waste of federal water supplies, curb water shortages, and lessen the need for costly new water projects, economists have suggested raising the price of federal water or, alternatively, allowing existing federal water users to sell their water rights to others or otherwise transfer such rights in order to distribute existing water supplies more efficiently.

DISCUSSION QUESTIONS

1. In your opinion, do the data presented in Table 6-1 refute the "water is different" philosophy?
2. If the price elasticity of demand for water in the short run and in the long run were equal, what would you expect to happen to the quantity of water demanded after a price increase?

part two
Market Structures

INTRODUCTION

Markets can take on many forms. The standard market structures that are usually discussed are (1) pure competition, (2) **monopolistic competition**, (3) **oligopoly**, and (4) **monopoly**. In this part, examples of these market structures are given.

An example of the perfectly competitive market is the market for publicly traded shares of common stock. It can be argued that such a market is extremely efficient, with the result that it is extremely difficult to "make a killing" by trading in that market, particularly if one uses **public information**. The monopolistically competitive market structure is illustrated by the economics of cents-off coupons. It is argued that retail food outlets are able to use price discrimination by means of cents-off coupons. Only in a situation of less-than-perfect competition could such price discrimination occur. The worlds of oligopoly and monopoly are illustrated by an analysis of ethical drug regulation, the medical industry, international cartels, state liquor monopolies, and cutthroat pricing.

One point should be kept in mind throughout this part: We are presenting models of human behavior, not of thought processes. Our analysis of the medical profession, for example, cannot be proved or disproved by asking physicians whether they think along the lines of our analysis. Our models are set up using an "as if" type of framework. That is to say, we assume that the individuals under study are acting as if they are attempting to maximize their own self-interest.

7

the economics of
The
Stock Market

Many people dream of becoming rich. Some will become rich in later years when they inherit wealth, that is, **stocks—common stock** or **preferred stock, bonds**, real estate, valuable paintings, and other kinds of property that their parents or relatives own. Most people, however, will not be so fortunate. To attain wealth, those individuals will have to work hard and put their **savings** into wise **investments**.

A distinction must be made here between putting savings into investments that will pay a steady rate of return year after year, and investing them in schemes to make a "killing" over the course of a few months or a year. Some individuals choose the latter course in an attempt to "get rich quick." Most people, however, do not gamble with their accumulated savings. Rather, they invest their savings in one or more of the following areas: savings accounts, long-term bonds, pension plans, and the stock market. Further, they usually leave most of their savings in the investment for 20–40 years before withdrawing it for retirement expenses.

There are, of course, many get-rich-quick schemes involving the stock market. One of the most popular is picking the "right" stocks to buy at the "right" time. But what are the right stocks and when is the right time? Obviously, they are stocks whose purchase price is currently low but whose selling price will be extremely high in time.

Perhaps your parents or friends deal in the stock market—that is, they buy and sell stock. If so, you have probably heard some strange words about "the market" in their conversations. They may talk about "hot" tips, or reasons why the market might rise or fall, or about a broker's forecasts of stock prices.

When one wants information about an illness, for example, one generally consults a doctor, or even goes to a specialist. If one wants information about how to repair a car, one may go to another type of specialist—an automobile mechanic. Thus, when seeking information about the stock market, logic would seem to suggest that one should go to a stock specialist—a broker.

This reasoning is partly accurate. A stockbroker can provide information about how the stock market operates and about the cost of buying and selling stocks. The broker can also lead the investor away from very risky stocks—those giving the investor small chance of making large gains but a large chance of losing everything. The broker can give advice concerning the right combination of stocks and bonds and can suggest different types of stocks for the investor's particular needs in terms of security and income in the future. But the broker is generally *not* the person who can make the investor rich quick. The broker *cannot* tell the investor, with absolute certainty, the best way to invest his or her dollars in the market.

Look in the Yellow Pages of the telephone book under "Stock and Bond Brokers" and pick a name at random. If you were to call one of the brokerage firms listed, you could ask to speak with a broker. (A broker is a salesperson, but he or she may have the title of "account executive.") The following example illustrates what would probably happen.

When you got the broker on the phone, you would tell him or her that you have $5000 to invest, and ask for advice. Before the broker tells you anything, he or she will ask you what your goals are. Do you want steady income from your investment of $5000? Do you want growth stocks that will provide a reasonable **capital gain** in the future?

After you tell the broker the strategy you want to take, he or she will probably advise you on the best stocks to buy and then predict (guess) whether the stock market will go up or down in the next few months. The broker's opinion will sound very informed and authoritative.

Strange as it may seem, though, the broker's advice on how to invest your money generally is not any better than anyone else's advice. In fact, *the chances of the broker's being right are no greater than the chances of your being right!* Does this sound improbable? Perhaps. Yet the fact remains that economists, statisticians, and investors have examined and tested this proposition from numerous angles. And all have reached the same conclusion.

You have probably never studied investing before. How can you guess about what the stock market will do? Or about how profitable a company may be in the future?

The stock market is one of the most competitive markets in the world. Competition among investors means that all investors try to do as well as they can. In doing so, each investor must compete with all other investors. Investors' efforts to gain higher profits are what make the stock market highly competitive. It is more competitive than most other markets because literally millions of investors trade in it. In addition, it is even more competitive because of the availability of information about it at relatively low cost.

Almost any daily newspaper will give you information about the price of stocks on the New York and major national stock exchanges as well as on certain regional stock exchanges. Stock price quotations are published daily in the financial section of the newspaper. In addition, current stock price information is available from most brokerage firms. These firms have tickertape-type electronic machines that receive price changes for various stocks almost as fast as they are announced, even though the firm may be more than 3000 miles from the stock exchange.

Information about a specific company also rapidly becomes widely known. As soon as a company announces its profits, literally millions of people learn about it. Such information is not as readily available as the prices of listed stocks, but it flows quite freely within the American economy.

The point is that by the time one investor reads about what a company, an industry, or, for that matter, the national economy is going to do, most other investors have also read it. The information is public information—available to anyone and everyone at very low cost. Public information cannot help you in your plan to get rich quick.

To understand why public information will not help, let us look at an example. Suppose a company in your neighborhood has discovered a substitute for gasoline. You read about the discovery in the newspaper. After reading the article, you decide the company's stock would be an excellent purchase because the company should make a great deal of money from its discovery.

But think about the idea more carefully. Will not everyone else think the same way? In fact, will not many people who learned about the discovery *before* you also realize that the company stands to make higher profits? Certainly they will. Some will already have bought stock in the company. As they bid against each other to buy stock, the price of the stock will start to rise. By the time you read about the discovery, competing investors will have *already* bid up the price of the stock to reflect the "new" information. Hence, by the time vital information becomes public, it is essentially useless to someone trying to get rich quick.

Because the stock market is so highly competitive and because information about it flows so freely, it follows a **random walk**. The market as a whole has trends, such as the general upward trend from its beginning that reflects, among other things, the reinvestment of company earnings. However, the prices of specific stocks and the average of all stock prices exhibit a random walk relative to the overall market trend. Any examination of past stock prices will not yield useful information for predicting future prices. Years of academic research have left little doubt that the stock market follows a random walk. If a person were to find out otherwise, he or she could get rich quickly.

Some individuals are superior forecasters of what will happen in the economy. They may have some special innate ability, or they may have developed a forecasting method that is superior to anyone else's. As long as the methods used by these individuals do not become common knowledge, these individuals can indeed make higher-than-normal profits in the stock market. It is the ability to *interpret* public information (and **inside information**, also) that gives some individuals the edge in the stock market.

SUMMARY

The market for publicly traded shares of stock is one of the most highly competitive in the world. Information about the future profitability of companies is quickly dispersed throughout the buying public. Therefore, that knowledge rarely, if ever, allows an individual to make a higher-than-normal rate of return in the stock market. The prices of stocks follow a random walk, and you cannot predict the future of the price of stocks by using past information. Only individuals with superior talents at interpreting public information have a chance to make a higher-than-normal rate of return, on average, in the stock market.

DISCUSSION QUESTIONS

1. The stock market is highly competitive. Therefore, what average rate of return can you predict you will make by "wheeling and dealing" in the stock market?
2. What is the value of public information?

the economics of
Cents-off Coupons

The producers of food and other products sold in the hundreds of thousands of retail food outlets across the United States frequently use "cents-off" coupons to attract customers. If these producers are competitive, why do they do so, since this practice is not consistent with a model of pure competition? Because the practice *is* consistent with a model of monopolistic competition, which allows for slight degrees of monopoly power by individual producers. We will show that the use of cents-off coupons is a form of price discrimination.

The full price of a product includes not only the monetary price but also the implicit opportunity cost of the time spent searching out the product and purchasing it (and the time needed to consume it). We can assume that, all else being equal, the higher one values time saved from shopping, the less time one will spend in seeking out lower-cost shopping arrangements. In other words, a person who places a higher value on time, relative to money, will spend more money to save shopping time. This means that a person who places a high value on time will exhibit a less elastic demand curve in a given store than a person who places a lower value on time.

Let us assume that there is a strong correlation between a person's wealth and the value he or she puts on time, that is, that richer people, on average, value their time more highly than do poorer people. It follows that a richer person's relative price **elasticity of demand** will be less than a poorer person's. Now the suppliers of the various products sold in retail food outlets are confronted with two classes of consumers: those with relatively less **elastic demand** and those with relatively more elastic demand. The supplier's problem is to separate these two classes and charge the richer customer a higher price than the poorer customer. One way that this can be (and is) done is to offer a rebate only to those customers who are willing to incur a time cost to obtain that rebate. The rebate is in the form of cents-off coupons, which are available only to those customers who take time to cut them out of magazines, keep track of them if they are received in the mail, or obtain them by some other means. These cents-off coupons must be kept with the person, taken to the retail food outlet, and then exchanged at the cash register for a reduction in the price charged for the particular item. All of these activities require time. Thus, poorer people, who we are assuming can be used as proxies for the relatively more elastic demanders, pay a lower money price for their purchases in retail food outlets when they utilize cents-off coupons. The richer customers, with relatively less elastic demand, refuse to be bothered by cents-off coupons because of the time cost involved, and as a result get no discount at all.

If the above cents-off coupon model is useful, it presents us with some testable implications.

1. We can predict that cents-off coupons will be offered relatively less often in cases where the price of a single purchase is large. This is because the receiver of a valuable coupon for a large purchase would incur a small time cost relative to the value of the coupon. In other words, not enough differential time costs would be imposed to discourage relatively low elasticity demanders from collecting the cents-off coupons. This implication is consistent with the fact that cents-off coupons are almost exclusively used for relatively low-priced items sold in retail food stores.

2. We can predict that when the commodity is a personal service, relatively few cents-off coupons will be used. The cents-off coupon is a substitute for price discounting, and the differentiation in quality of services offered already accomplishes the price-discriminating goal. This implication is consistent with the observation that beauty parlors and barber shops typically do not give cents-off coupons.

SUMMARY

Even in the competitive world of retail food, each retailer has a slight amount of market power. In other words, monopolistic competition prevails. In order to exploit their slight market power, individual sellers offer cents-off coupons. This allows them to price discriminate, effectively offering lower prices to individuals who place a lower value on their time and higher prices to individuals who place a higher value on their time. In general, the former are poorer customers and the latter are richer customers.

DISCUSSION QUESTIONS

1. Why is monopolistic competition the appropriate model for food producers? Does it seem to be the

appropriate model for other industries? Why or why not?

2. How does the use of cents-off coupons allow the monopolistic competitor to price discriminate among customers with different price elasticities of demand?

the economics of
Drug Regulation

Medical drugs are a two-edged sword. If they are carefully manufactured, appropriate for curing your illness, and free of side effects, your pain and suffering may be prevented, or at least assuaged. If, on the other hand, the drug you happen to take under your doctor's supervision turns out to have side effects, you may be worse off than if you had never taken the drug at all, or if you had taken an alternative drug without side effects. Federal regulation has been concerned not only with the safety, but also with the efficacy—the effectiveness—of drugs for many years. The first federal legislation, the Food and Drug Act of 1906, dealt with adulteration and misbranding. Safety was also covered under the adulteration section. That act prohibited inclusion of any substance that would be poisonous or harmful to health. To some extent, the act was successful. Dr. Hostetter's celebrated Stomach Bitters and Kickapoo Indian Sagwa, along with numerous rum-laden concoctions and anticancer remedies, disappeared from the alchemists' shelves as a result of this legislation. The original act was expanded in 1938 with the passage of the federal Food, Drug, and Cosmetic Act, which forced manufacturers to demonstrate the safety of new drugs. It resulted from public reaction to the deaths of 107 individuals who had taken an elixir of sulfanilamide. This was the chemical compound sulfanilamide dissolved in diethylene glycol, which is a poisonous substance usually used as antifreeze.

The next big public outrage came after the birth of numerous deformed infants whose mothers had been taking a sleeping pill called Thalidomide. At the time that these deformities were publicized, the Food and Drug Administration (FDA) was actually moving toward approving Thalidomide in the United States. About two-and-a-half million Thalidomide tablets were in the hands of physicians as samples. At the insistence of President John F. Kennedy, the FDA removed all of the samples. Using the Thalidomide scandal as ammunition, Senator Estes Kefauver secured passage of his bill, known as the 1962 Kefauver-Harris Amendments to the 1938 Food, Drug, and Cosmetic Act. Kefauver and his associates wished to prevent, among other things, a proliferation of new drugs. Prior to the 1962 amendments, the FDA normally approved a new drug application within 180 days, unless the application did not adequately demonstrate during that time that the drug was safe for use as suggested in the proposed labeling. The 1962 amendments added a "proof of efficacy" requirement and removed the time constraint on the FDA. Thus, since 1962, it has been the case that no drug can be marketed unless and until the FDA determines that it is safe and effective in its intended use.

Let's reiterate here what is at issue. Legislation has been passed and the FDA enforces it so that two things are prevented: (1) the marketing of unsafe drugs, and (2) the proliferation of drugs that are "unnecessary" in the sense that similar efficacy could be obtained by older, already tested drugs. Consumers presumably are better protected by this legislation because generally they do not have the ability to obtain (let alone fully analyze) the information necessary to make an accurate choice about the safety or efficacy of a particular drug. They are, in a sense, at the mercy of their physicians. But their physicians are also, in a sense, at the mercy of the drug companies. Physicians cannot possibly keep up with the technical literature about drugs and comprehend the differences among them. To keep the medical profession informed, drug companies spend thousands of dollars a year per physician. They send out so-called detail people to inform physicians of new drugs and to give them samples to dispense to patients, so doctors can find out for themselves how effective the drugs really are. To be sure, doctors, hospitals, and drug companies do have an incentive to prescribe, market, and produce safe drugs. After all, if it can be proven that side effects from drug use cause harm to an individual, the ensuing lawsuit will certainly make the doctor, hospital, and/or manufacturer worse off. Additionally, the negative publicity surrounding such a lawsuit will not enhance the future reputation of the drug company involved. And finally, the more lawsuits filed and won by injured parties, the higher the total cost of production of drugs and the higher the price ultimately paid by the consumer. Assuming there is at least some price elasticity of demand for drugs (that it is not zero), the resultant higher price to the consumer will cause a reduction in the quantity demanded.

The 1962 amendments seem to have been very effective, given that the number of new drugs introduced into the medical marketplace has been drastically reduced. From 1961 to 1962, the number of new chemical entities and new drugs introduced was about 340. From 1963 to 1970, when the Kefauver Amendments were in effect, the number dropped to an average of 110 annually. That should not be surprising. The cost of introducing a new drug has risen dramatically. Prior to the 1962 amendments, the average time between filing and approval of a new drug application was 7 months; by 1967, it was 30 months; and currently it takes 8–10 years for a new drug to be approved by the FDA. In other words, the 1962 amendments have resulted in extending the period during which new drugs must be continuously tested. In making investment decisions, firms are keenly aware of this additional cost.

The effect of such costs has been what some people call the U.S. drug lag. The number of drugs marketed in England that are not available in the United States, for example, is very much larger than the reverse situation.

Now we come to the realization that for every benefit. there seems to be a cost. Clearly, there is a dollar cost to the drug companies in testing more completely the efficacy and safety of a drug. But if that were the only issue, there probably wouldn't be many critics of the FDA. The reason there are so many critics today is the cost to individuals, who might be better off if more drugs had been introduced into the United States since 1962.

Let's now consider the safety problem in total. Every time a new drug is introduced, it has potentially harmful side effects. Thus, part of the cost of introducing that drug is the cost of the undesired side effects to those who incur them. This is called a "Type I error." It is the probability of being wrong, that is, of having introduced a drug that should not have been introduced. Since 1962, we have reduced the Type I error—the Thalidomide possibility—by increasing the amount of testing necessary for the introduction of new drugs. People have undoubtedly benefited by this reduction in Type I error by incurring fewer side effects. But other people have been hurt. They have been the victims of what is called a "Type II error." Their cost is the pain, suffering, and possible death that occur because of the lack of availability of a drug that *would have been offered* on the marketplace in the absence of the 1962 amendments. The Type II error, then, is the probability of not introducing new drugs that should have been introduced. To understand better the cost of a Type II error, consider the possibility of the 1962 drug amendments being applied to aspirin. It is very hard to demonstrate *why* aspirin is effective—and it may have bad side effects, such as duodenal ulcers, if taken often. Imagine, though, if it had never been introduced. What would the cost have been? People would have incurred more pain from headaches, arthritis, and so on. In other words, the Type II error cost is the pain and suffering that occur because a drug was *not* introduced.

In some cases, the FDA has shortened the testing period for drugs in cases where Type I errors are insignificant compared to Type II errors—as is the case with terminally ill individuals. Since the mid-1970s, the FDA has approved several drugs on the basis of a shorter testing period for use in the treatment of patients with terminal diseases. A vaccine for use in the treatment of AIDS (acquired immune deficiency syndrome) emerged in 1986 with tentative FDA approval after only a two-year testing period. When it was found that azidothymidine (AZT) prolonged the lives of patients with AIDS, it was felt that the possible side effects of the drug (Type I errors)—such as headaches, nausea, and a reduction in the number of disease-fighting white blood cells—could hardly be balanced against the many deaths (Type II errors) that would result if the drug weren't quickly approved.

Recently, the FDA has also shortened the period of time necessary for the approval of **generic drugs**. In cases where a generic drug is of essentially the same composition of a drug formerly approved and marketed under a brand name, upon expiration of the patent held by the original producer the FDA allows the drug to be marketed under its generic name with little further testing.

SUMMARY

The regulation of the ethical drug market has had long-run effects. It is impossible to reduce the probability of undesired side effects from new drugs without increasing the probability that fewer beneficial drugs will be available to help those who need them. In statistical terms, this is called the **tradeoff** between a Type I and a Type II error. In a world of scarce resources, this tradeoff always exists. If we wanted to eliminate all Type I errors—that is, all negative side effects—we could make all ethical drugs illegal. But the cost in terms of Type II errors—the loss of all the drugs that help alleviate pain and suffering, and postpone death—would be enormous.

DISCUSSION QUESTIONS

1. Does the type of market structure in which drugs are produced have anything to do with the tradeoff between Type I and Type II errors? In other words, would our analysis be different if the drug industry were either perfectly competitive or a pure monopoly?

2. On the whole, do you feel longer testing periods for drugs by the FDA have increased or reduced the amount of pain and suffering experienced in the United States?

10

the economics of
Rising
Medical Costs

Most people don't have to be told about how expensive it is these days to see a doctor or to go into a hospital. If we compare the **Consumer Price Index** (CPI) with a medical care price index, we see that since 1967 the CPI has increased by 327 percent, while the medical care index has increased by 422 percent. We spent only $4 billion on medical care in 1929; we increased our spending to $40 billion by 1965; and today it is over $400 billion. In 1929, expenditures on medical care represented only 4 percent of total national spending, but today's expenditures represent 11 percent. We can say, therefore, that as real income rises, Americans demand not just more medical care, but more in proportion to their rising incomes.[1]

[1]In other words, the **income elasticity of demand** for medical care exceeds 1.

If we wish to understand why medical care is so expensive, we have to look at a number of factors. They include (1) past restrictions on the supply of physicians, (2) increases in demand created by Medicare and Medicaid, (3) increases in the quantity of care demanded due to third-party insurance, and (4) soaring medical malpractice insurance costs and resultant increases in so-called defensive medicine.

Entry into the medical profession is by no means unrestricted. Latest figures show, for example, that about 33,000 people take the standard medical school admissions test and only 16,000 are accepted. The number of applicants to Harvard's medical school runs to almost 3500, but the class size remains at less than 150. Some students apply to as many as 10 different medical schools and when turned down reapply two or three times. The number of students who don't apply because they know the odds are so much against them is probably two or three times the number of those who take the chance. Moreover, many applicants don't get into medical school because the number of medical schools in the United States is severely restricted.

In principle, they are restricted as a result of state licensing requirements, which universally prohibit proprietary medical schools (schools run for profit). A medical school must be accredited by the state for its graduates to be allowed to take the licensing exam required for practicing medicine. If we look back to the first decade of this century, we find that there were 192 medical schools in the United States. By 1944, that number had declined to 69. The number of physicians per 100,000 people dropped from 157 in 1900 to 132 in 1957. The reason for these precipitous declines was the success of the American Medical Association in controlling the output of doctors.

The regulation and certification of medical schools were based on the findings of the so-called Flexner Report. In 1910, the prestigious Carnegie Foundation commissioned

Abraham Flexner[2] to inspect the existing medical education facilities in the United States. Flexner's recommendations resulted in the demise of half of the then-existing medical schools.[3] It is interesting to note that Flexner (himself not a physician or even a scientist) was examining the *inputs* and not the *outputs* of the schools. Instead of finding out how well or how qualified the *graduates* of the different schools were, he looked at how they were taught. This is equivalent to your instructor giving you a grade on the basis of how many hours you spent studying rather than how well you did on the final exam.

The purpose of the stricture on medical schools was described by the former head of the AMA's Council on Medical Education, who said in 1928 that

> the reduction of the number of medical schools from 160 to 80 (resulted in) a marked reduction in number of medical students and medical graduates. We had anticipated this and felt that this was a desirable thing. We had . . . a great oversupply of poor and mediocre practitioners.

In economic terms, the supply curve shifted inward as the demand curve either remained stable or shifted outward. The result was that the price of physicians' services went up, thereby allowing them to make higher incomes. The census of 1970, for example, showed that physicians had the highest income of any profession.[4] In that year, it was on average $41,500, at a time when self-employed dentists earned $28,100, engineers $17,700, and college full profes-

[2]Flexner was a historian whose brother was the Johns Hopkins University medical dean. The model Flexner used to judge the "quality" of all other medical schools was the medical school at Johns Hopkins.
[3]Some medical historians believe that before 1900, doctors probably killed more people than they cured. The Carnegie Foundation and the American Medical Association certainly had legitimate concerns about the quality of medical care at that time.
[4]Part of this is due, however, to longer average hours worked per week.

sors $16,800. In 1974, the median net income of physicians who incorporated themselves was $72,500. Today physicians remain the highest-paid professionals, with an average annual income of $110,000.

We can ask ourselves whether the AMA's avowed wishes were satisfied. The AMA maintained that the qualifications of many doctors were deficient—that the public was being serviced by doctors who were doing damage to unsuspecting patients. The idea behind medical school licensing was to weed out the most unqualified students and to eliminate the possibility of an unsuspecting sick person being treated by an inadequately trained, yet licensed, doctor. It is strange, though, that the AMA did not seek in 1910 to analyze the qualifications of the current crop of physicians. The closure of one-half of the medical schools resulted in the elimination of the *future* supply of supposedly unqualified doctors, but the supposedly unqualified doctors who were already in practice were allowed to continue practicing until retirement or death.

It is possible, too, that the *quality* of medical care consumed by the public did not increase as much as the AMA professed it did after the closure of half of the medical schools. After all, there are two kinds of medical services. One is self-diagnosis and self-treatment; the other is relying on someone in the medical care industry. If the price of a physician's diagnosis and treatment goes up, then one might expect that the quantity demanded would fall, and an increased reliance on self-diagnosis and self-treatment would result. People would go to doctors only after their symptoms became alarming. It may be, then, that the increase in the quality—and therefore the price—of doctors' services resulted in in a *decrease* in the *total* quality of medical care utilized, because doctors were consulted less often. Moreover, when the price of the services of licensed physicians goes up, there is an increase in the demand for substitute healing services, and these substitutes may well be inferior to even a poorly trained M.D.

Concurrently with the restriction on the supply of physicians in the United States, there have been, at times, dramatic increases in demand, which have brought about rising prices. Certain government programs have shifted the demand curve to the right. One of these programs is Medicare, free medical care for the aged. Prior to Medicare, congressional estimates of what that program would cost were many times less than what the actual cost turned out to be. This can be easily explained, since the demand for medical services is responsive to the price charged. When Medicare was instituted, in the mid-1960s, the actual price of health care services to many people was drastically lowered. As the price fell, the quantity demanded rose—so much so that the available supply of medical services was taxed beyond capacity. The only thing that could give was the price, and it gave. Hospital room charges skyrocketed after the imposition of Medicare and its state counterpart, Medicaid.[5]

Similar in their effects are medical insurance plans rooted in the private sector of the economy. At least 180 million Americans are covered by some private medical insurance. Generally this insurance pays a percentage of hospital expenses. Herein lies a problem: Insurance usually covers more inpatient services than outpatient services. Individuals covered by insurance therefore, have an incentive to go to a hospital to be taken care of by their private doctors, and their private doctors have an incentive to send them there in order to collect payment. And, as with Medicare and Medicaid, private insurance plans increase the quantity of services demanded simply because the direct out-of-pocket costs are very low or zero. The insurance industry has a term for this—moral hazard. In economics, we translate this term into a demand curve that slopes downward (i.e., the quantity of services demanded increases when the

---

[5]Doctors began to order just as many expensive tests for their poor Medicare patients as they did for their rich patients.

price falls).[6] Many medical services could be postponed or never used at all; for example, cosmetic surgery and, to a lesser extent, other elective surgery. But the lower the price charged, the more cosmetic and elective surgery will be undertaken. And the lower the price, the more likely people are to visit their doctors when they have a slight ailment, such as a cold. In other words, when people are directly charged the full price of their physicians' services, they are likely to use them more sparingly. But if the price is reduced to practically zero, some of them (at least those on the margin) will respond by seeing their physicians for minor ailments.

Furthermore, because of third-party insurance, doctors, in conjunction with hospitals, have been ordering more and more tests, using more and more advanced techniques. Hospitals have an incentive to use the most exotic techniques possible and doctors to order them, knowing full well that patients will be reimbursed by their insurance companies for a large percentage of the cost. The problem is that patients covered by insurance do not pay the *direct* cost of the medical care they receive in a hospital at the time they receive it. Obviously, they pay eventually through higher premiums, but that cost is spread out over everyone who buys the insurance. The result is that the quantity of services demanded in the hospital will be more than it otherwise would be. This causes hospital expenses to go up, all other things held constant.

Another reason for the high cost of medical care has been increasing malpractice costs. Individuals are suing their doctors and hospitals more than ever before, and juries are awarding larger amounts to malpractice victims each year—the average amount reaching the $1-million mark in 1985. In 1978, 3 percent of American doctors were sued for malprac-

[6]Of course, the full price, including the insurance premium, does not fall—it rises. But the insurance premium is a fixed cost. It does not vary with the number of visits to the doctor or trips to the hospital.

tice; six years later, in 1984, 16 percent of physicians were sued, and the number continues to climb. Increased malpractice premiums for doctors have resulted: On average, malpractice insurance premiums have risen 32 percent per year over the past several years. Skyrocketing malpractice insurance costs for health-care providers have been passed on to the consumer in the form of higher prices for health-care services and more extensive testing, evaluation procedures, and consultations undertaken by physicians to prevent the possibility of lawsuit. According to the Harvard School of Public Health, Americans paid a staggering $42 billion just for this "defensive medicine" in 1986. Because of caps set on malpractice awards in many states, further soaring of malpractice costs may be curbed in the future, however.

We end this chapter with a discussion of the future supply of medical-care personnel. Ironically, after decades of experiencing a shortage of doctors, the reverse is apparently soon to be the case. If current estimates are correct, by the year 1990 there will be between 70,000 and 185,000 "surplus" doctors.

What has caused this turnaround in the supply of doctors? For one thing, the shortage of doctors in the past two decades and the consequent high incomes in that profession drew the maximum number to the medical field. Notwithstanding the difficulty of entering—and paying for—medical school, there has been a gradual increase in the number of graduates in the past several years. In addition, Americans going abroad for medical training and the immigration of foreign doctors have helped to increase the supply of physicians relative to the population from 1 doctor for every 697 Americans in 1965 to 1 doctor for every 471 Americans in 1986.

At the same time, there has been an increase in the number of alternative health-care providers (such as nurse practitioners, midwives, and paramedical services) that now perform some of the functions formerly carried out only by medical doctors. Also, employers who find it hard to pay for employees' medical benefits are increasingly turning to preferred-provider organizations (PPOs) and other prepaid health plans that deliver employee medical care to employers at a lower cost. Competition from such plans seriously jeopardizes the continuing high incomes of standard fee-for-service medical practices.

Physicians who wish to pursue private practices are now facing, for the first time in decades, the problem of luring sufficient patients to their services to make a "good" living. High malpractice insurance costs, a greater supply of doctors, and the rapid development of lower-cost health-care alternatives have introduced a larger element of competition into the medical profession. Although it has never been easy for a young doctor to establish a medical practice, it is now a much more difficult undertaking. Marketing seminars in the study of selling tactics are now being taken by a number of physicians. Advertising, which became legal for the medical profession several years ago, is now more frequently resorted to by doctors, especially those just setting up a private medical practice, as are house calls, evening hours, and weekend availability. Some doctors even offer special conveniences to their patients, such as beepers for them to carry while waiting for their appointments—so they can carry on shopping or other activities until their turn comes—or TVs in waiting rooms to make delays more palatable. Obviously, the laws of supply and demand still operate, even in the medical-care profession.

SUMMARY

The high cost of medical care in this country stems from a mixture of past restrictions on supply, soaring demand as a consequence of zero or below-market prices for Medicare and Medicaid patients, third-party insurance, and the increasing number of malpractice suits. A growing supply of doctors, however, and an increasing number of health-care alternatives and providers give evidence that the laws of supply and demand operate in the medical profession as well and that costs for health care may be reduced in the future.

DISCUSSION QUESTIONS

1. The more opportunity individuals have to pass medical care costs on to third parties such as insurance companies, the less incentive they have to take care of themselves. The insurance industry calls this a problem of moral hazard. Is there any way this problem can be resolved to help reduce medical care costs?
2. Until relatively recently, doctors were not allowed to advertise their services. Even since then, some physicians have felt that the advertising of medical-care services is unethical. Do you agree?

11

the economics of
International Cartels

Every week 300 of the world's richest and most prestigious diamond dealers are invited to view the "sights" in an office on Fleet Street in London. These sights are uncut diamonds being sold by the Central Selling Organization, or CSO. The CSO's nine-story office building in London is popularly known as "the syndicate." Through it every year passes 80 percent of the supply of rough-cut diamonds in the world. One organization controls that 80 percent of the supply—DeBeers, the famous diamond company. In 1978, it marketed $2.5 billion worth of gems, a 23 percent increase over 1977. DeBeers also produces about 35 percent of the world's diamonds. It's clearly in a good monopoly position. The 300 diamond dealers who come in every week are shown the diamonds and told the price. Haggling is essentially not allowed; in fact, it is rumored that if one haggles, one is not asked back.

If DeBeers were simply the producer of 35 percent of the world's diamonds, it might not have such an effective control on the market price of diamonds; but it has been successful in forming a very strong **cartel**-type arrangement in which it is the sole marketing agent of another 45 percent of the world's rough-cut diamonds. In this way it becomes an effective monopoly: It controls the sales, or more specifically the amount of sales, that are offered to diamond dealers throughout the world. It can effectively police the number of diamonds offered for sale every year. It can do what a monopolist wishes to do—restrict output and thereby raise the price above what it would be in a perfectly competitive situation.

Another successful international cartel is OPEC, the Organization of Petroleum Exporting Countries. In 1960, OPEC started as an organization designed to assist the oil-exporting countries. By 1970 it included Abu Dhabi, Algeria, Indonesia, Iran, Iraq, Kuwait, Libya, Nigeria, Qatar, Saudi Arabia, and Venezuela; since then a few other countries, including Ecuador, have joined the group, and other nations have left the cartel. During the 1960s OPEC's success was limited because an ever-expanding supply of oil kept just ahead of demand. As demand grew, new discoveries expanded the supplies so fast that nominal well-head prices for crude oil actually fell slightly between 1960 and 1970. Then in 1970 and 1971, the rate of growth of the demand for crude oil tapered off. Also in 1970, Libya, which had become a major supplier of crude oil to Western European markets, had a revolution. The new regime cut output sharply in a partly political move against the oil companies to which concessions had been granted by the previous regime. Libya's cutback made sizable price increases possible in 1971. These increases were ratified by the other members of OPEC in agreements drawn up in Tripoli and Teheran.

Much of the success of this rise in prices was credited to OPEC, although some observers contend that Libya was alone responsible and had no help from OPEC.

The main ingredient in OPEC's success, however, was the outbreak of war in the Middle East in 1973. In the wake of this war, Saudi Arabia, Kuwait, and a few smaller Arab countries agreed to cut back greatly their production of crude oil, thus paving the way for large price increases. Remember that the only way to raise prices when one is a pure monopolist is to cut back on production and sales. Thus, OPEC members could have an effective cartel arrangement only if some or all of them cut back on production and sales. Since Saudi Arabia, which accounts for the bulk of the oil production in the Middle East, did cut back greatly in 1973, the cartel arrangement worked, and it contined to work for several years. The total profits for the oil-exporting countries were increased greatly as a result.

The effect of OPEC cartelization activities on world oil prices was dramatic. On January 1, 1973, one could buy Saudi Arabian crude oil at $2.12 a barrel. Within one year, the price of crude had risen to $7.61 per barrel; by 1975, to $10.50; and by 1978, to $14.57.

Other international cartels have been formed, many of them involved with internationally traded commodities. The International Bauxite Association (IBA) has attempted to control the price of bauxite around the world. The International Tin Agreement has existed since before World War II. The Organization of Banana-Exporting Countries has tried to duplicate OPEC's success. There are producer cartels in iron ore, mercury, tea, tropical timber, natural rubber, nickel, cobalt, tungsten, columbium, pepper, tantalum, and quinine, and probably many more. Not all of them are successful. We now ask the question: What are the necessary ingredients to a successful cartel arrangement?

A cartel must meet four basic requirements if it is to be successful:

1. It must control a large share of total actual output and potential. It must not face substantial competition from outsiders.
2. Available substitutes must be limited. In other words, the price elasticity of demand for the product in question must be fairly low; that is, there must be relatively (but not completely) **inelastic demand**.
3. The demand for the cartel's product must be relatively stable, regardless of business conditions. If this is not the case, then the amount sold at any given price will be greater during economic **expansions** than during recessions, and the cartel will find it difficult to maintain any given price and output combination for very long.
4. Producers must be willing and able to withhold sufficient amounts of their product to affect the market. Each member must resist the temptation to cheat. And consumers must not be able to have large stockpiles of the product on which to draw.

There are probably other conditions that would make a cartel's success probability even greater, but these can be considered the basic ones.

A big cause of cartel instability is cheating. When there are many firms or countries in a cartel arrangement, there will always be some that are unhappy with the situation. They will want to cheat by charging a slightly lower price than the one stipulated by the cartel. Members who are producing a small percentage of the total output of the cartel essentially face a very elastic demand curve if they cheat and no one else does. A small drop in price by a cheater will result in a very large increase in total revenues.

There will always be cartel members who figure that it will pay them to cut prices. Each firm will try to do this, thinking that the others will not do the same thing. Or a firm may decide that other firms are going to cheat anyway, so why shouldn't it be the first? Obviously, though, when a sufficient number of firms in the cartel try to cheat, the cartel breaks up. We would expect, therefore, that as long as the cartel is not maintained by legislation, there will be a constant threat to its existence. Its members will have a large incentive to cut prices, and once a couple of members do that, the rest may follow.

Consider, for example, the failure of the copper cartel, CIPEC, the Intergovernmental Council of Copper Exporting Countries. CIPEC was founded in 1967 by Chile, Zambia, Zaire, and Peru. It still exists, but it has never managed to show any muscle in world markets. In 1974 the price of copper started falling. From April to the end of December, it had dropped by 55 percent. CIPEC was powerless to bring it back up. Why? Because most of the developing countries are unwilling or unable to limit their output of copper. There isn't a Saudi Arabia of the copper world that is willing to cut back 50 percent on production so that the rest of the cartel can enjoy higher prices. Remember, the only way to keep prices up is to keep production down.

The coffee cartel hasn't fared much better. The price of coffee has gone up and down like a yoyo. Every time the price starts falling, big coffee producers such as Colombia and Brazil urge other producing nations to cut back. They do so at the annual meeting of the Council of International Coffee Organization (ICO). Moreover, ICO has found out what the price elasticity of demand for coffee really is. Each time the price has jumped, the quantity demanded has fallen, sometimes dramatically. In 1977, for example, the general manager of Colombia's coffee growers' federation thought that the 60-cent increase per pound on the average in retail prices during the last two years had caused consumption to drop by 15 percent. His suggestion to other coffee producers at that time? Lower prices. In other words, even a strong cartel cannot face up to the possibility of consumers cutting back on the consumption of a higher-priced good.

Cartel instability, or lack of success, is not confined to business firms or even to nations engaging in international commodities selling. Have you ever noticed how short-lived a homemakers' boycott of a supermarket is? There are so many members in that particular cartel that it is difficult for one of them not to "cheat" and actually go out and buy some food from the supermarket. It is impossible to police the large number of homemakers involved.

Consider one more example, which is hypothetical. If you are in a class of 100 students whose exams will be graded on a curve, how easily could all of you get together and agree to cut down study time? Would your cartel be successful? The answer, of course, depends on each individual student's incentive to cheat. If only one student were to cheat and study longer than all the others, that student would get a higher grade than he or she would otherwise have received. If enough students do this, the cartel will break down.

Several of the cartels discussed in this chapter are under serious pressure at the writing of this edition. The DeBeers diamond cartel has been singularly unsuccessful in keeping the price of diamonds from falling. Starting in 1980, the demand for all collectibles and so-called real, or hard, assets fell dramatically as individuals, particularly in the United States, no longer sought inflation hedges. Moreover, there was a worldwide recession starting in 1981. In spite of a reduction in the quantity of diamonds supplied to the market, the wholesale price of diamonds fell by over 60 percent from their historical highs at the end of the 1970s. Perhaps the biggest blow to the diamond cartel, however, was Australia's new Ashton mine, which has added an estimated 40 percent to world diamond production. Perhaps DeBeers will be successful in also controlling the output of that diamond supply, but if it is not, the cartel may collapse.

The OPEC cartel was also unsuccessful in keeping the price of crude oil at historically high levels. In March of 1983, for the first time in its 23-year history, OPEC agreed to cut the prices of its crude oil. The many years of relatively high prices finally had their effect: The worldwide supply of oil increased dramatically over the 10-year period from the first "energy crisis" in 1973. The cartel is currently having trouble deciding upon a unified response to the fall in oil prices because the smaller nation-members are unwilling to cut production—which could raise the price—because they think they need to continue to produce at current levels in order to sustain their oil revenues. The cartel has also been weakened by its inability to attract major producers, such as Mexico, into the cartel.

SUMMARY

Cartel arrangements are methods by which cartel members restrict supply in order to keep prices high. After all, the law of demand states that price and quantity demanded are inversely related. There is no way to sell the same quantity at a higher price, other things held constant. Therefore, potential cartel founders must realize that they must be successful in restricting output in order to raise prices. Several cartels have done just that, among them the diamond cartel and the oil cartel. In all cartel arrangements, there is an incentive for cartel members to cheat. Provided that they can cheat without being detected, they will make a higher profit. When all cartel members simultaneously attempt to cheat and are effective in so doing, the cartel breaks down and prices fall.

DISCUSSION QUESTIONS

1. Why are all cartels inherently unstable?
2. Would it be easier to form a cartel in a market with many producers or one with very few producers?

12

the economics of
The High Cost of Alcohol

Buying alcohol, particuarly so-called hard alcohol, is often an expensive proposition. Relative to many other beverages, comparable-sized bottles of scotch, bourbon, gin, vodka, and the like are many times more expensive. To be sure, compared to other beverages, the process of producing certain types of alcoholic beverages is more costly, as are the ingredients. But there is another major reason why alcohol is more expensive compared to other beverages, and that is because it is taxed so heavily. Indeed, in some states as much as 70 percent or more of the total price of a bottle of spirits can consist of various federal and state taxes.

In addition to differences in state tax laws, there is another important reason why alcoholic beverages cost more in certain states than in others. Differentiations in price also have to do with the ownership of the stores that sell alcohol.

In the United States, wholesale and retail distribution of liquor takes place in two forms: (1) via state-government monopoly, and (2) via privately owned firms that have purchased licenses to sell alcohol wholesale and retail. As of 1984, 15 states geographically scattered around the United States had complete control over liquor sales. In each of those 15 states, a state agency buys liquor and sells it through state-owned and operated stores. In the remainder of the states, private business firms compete for the liquor trade.

Economic theory suggests that monopoly creates a higher price than competition. If this is true, one would expect to find that the cost of liquor is higher in those states where liquor is controlled and distributed by state-owned stores. But is this the case?

A study done in 1980 by the Distilled Spirits Council of the United States concluded that, on the contrary, in states where liquor sales were controlled by state agencies, the price of liquor was actually slightly lower. One might contend then, that the theory of monopoly predicts incorrectly, at least in the case of liquor stores.

But is the actual *money* price in state-controlled liquor stores the *full* price? The answer is no, because the nature of price is such that the full price of liquor includes the value of the *time* it takes to find a store, the time it takes to purchase the liquor, the amount of help that is provided in the store, the ability to purchase liquor with checks and credit cards, and the other convenience factors, such as the number of hours that the store is open.

Consider just one such convenience factor—how long it takes to find a store as measured by the number of stores available per unit of population in each state. Holding income, liquor prices, and population density constant, the number of stores per capita is much higher in the private-ownership states than in the public-ownership states. The number of persons per liquor store outlet in the monopoly states is 10 times the number of persons per liquor store outlet in the nonmonopoly states. Clearly, it is on average much easier to find a liquor store—it is closer to home—in nonmonopoly states than in monopoly states.

Now consider the amount of help that is given to the person who enters a liquor store in the two situations. The average salary check per sales clerk in the monopoly-ownership states is about 40 percent higher than in the private-ownership states. As one would expect, to offset the higher wage costs in the public-ownership states, the stores there hire fewer workers relative to sales than do the private-ownership states. Consequently, one can predict that the amount of sales clerk help provided in public ownership states is less.

In continuing the study of the differences in convenience factors, it has been found that privately owned stores generally carry a larger selection of brands, accept checks and credit cards, and are open longer hours and more days of the year.

Monopoly theory predicts that price should be higher and output lower in monopoly situations. In the case of liquor stores, when the *full* price of liquor is considered, monopoly theory makes an accurate prediction.

SUMMARY

Monopoly theory suggests that a monopoly will charge a higher price for a particular product than it would obtain in a situation where competition exists. At first glance, this theory would seem to be called into question by the fact that in the 15 states where the state monopolizes liquor distribution and sales, the average money price of alcohol is slightly less than it is in the states where liquor is sold by privately owned businesses in a competitive environment. In fact, however, the full price paid at the state-controlled liquor stores is greater when "hidden costs" such as accessibility, customer service, and convenience are taken into account.

DISCUSSION QUESTIONS

1. What economic argument can you make for maintaining state-controlled liquor stores?
2. Do you think state-run liquor stores could exist side by side with privately run stores and still make a profit?

13

the economics of
Cutthroat Pricing

The words *cutthroat* and *predatory* are meant to be harsh. They conjure up in the reader's or listener's mind either a killer slitting someone's throat or a vicious animal pouncing on its prey. When these terms are applied to pricing, the image of a large business overwhelming a small, "defenseless" business comes to mind.

The term **cutthroat**, or **predatory, pricing** was first used by an economist to explain how an aggressive business firm could become a monopoly. Predatory pricing involves selling at a loss—presumably selling below **marginal cost**—in order to cause competitors to continue to lose money until they are forced to leave the marketplace and, it is hoped, sell what is left of their businesses to the predatory-pricing culprit. Once these competing firms are eliminated from the market, the cutthroat-pricing instigator can then raise prices and obtain monopoly profits. In the industrial history of the United States, a number of large firms have been accused of cutthroat pricing, including the Standard Oil trust in the late 1800s, which was dissolved by the Supreme Court in 1911. During the era of Franklin D. Roosevelt's New Deal in the 1930s, it was commonly assumed by many Americans that big businesses consistently engaged in predatory pricing.

Antitrust legislation in the United States prohibits monopolizing practices and specifically prohibits sellers from cutting prices to levels substantially below costs—that is, predatory pricing. But the distinction between simply cutting prices to increase competition and cutthroat, or predatory, pricing is sometimes a difficult one for the courts to draw.

In recent years, lawyers of firms facing rivalry, particularly from the Japanese, have looked to the courts for assistance in removing these competitors from the market on the basis of antitrust laws. The courts, however, have tended to look at the marketing of low-cost Japanese goods in the United States as a competitive, not a monopolizing, practice. Such was the case, for example, in the recently decided Supreme Court case *Matsushita Electric et al. v. Zenith.*[1]

In 1974, lawyers for Zenith Corporation, the electronics firm, used the predatory-pricing **model** to justify an antitrust case against 21 Japanese television makers. Zenith contended that the Japanese were using cutthroat pricing to monopolize the U.S. market and that the Japanese had conspired for the past 20 years to sell televisions in the United States below cost. In the spring of 1986 (court cases do move slowly!), the U.S. Supreme Court rejected Zenith's claim. The Court found that the two largest American producers of television tubes, Zenith and RCA, still controlled 40 percent of the U.S. television market, the same percentage that they had controlled in the 1970s. Also, the notion that 21 television makers anywhere in the world would consistently

[1]106 S. Ct. 1348 (1986).

sell products at below cost over a 20-year period seemed patently absurd. The justices concluded that "the claim is one that simply makes no economic sense."

In the *Zenith* decision, the Supreme Court clearly sent a message to American businesses: Don't use antitrust laws to discourage competition. As Justice Powell wrote in his decision, "Cutting price in order to increase business is the very essence of competition." Indeed, Justice Powell warned the lower courts to dismiss quickly all predatory-pricing cases unless there is real evidence of conspiracy.

Just because Zenith lost its cutthroat-pricing case doesn't mean its lawyers have to go home. They can now work on the $1-billion lawsuit they have filed against the Japanese television makers for "dumping." **Dumping** is a term used to describe a practice on the international market whereby producers sell products abroad at prices lower than those charged domestically. In principle, dumping requires that a firm charge higher prices at home in order to subsidize the low-cost sales abroad until the desired share of the foreign market is obtained. Foreign firms would dump in the United States only if they thought that in the long run they could increase profits enough to compensate for the reduced profits during the period of dumping. In the meantime, of course, there is at least one group of beneficiaries of such purported dumping—American consumers. Indeed, there are even proponents of dumping (if, in fact, it exists) who argue that U.S. consumers benefit by the lower-priced commodities and are always willing to get a good deal. If foreign firms wish to subsidize American consumers, so be it—or at least so goes the argument.

U.S. silicon chip manufacturers are another group accusing the Japanese of dumping. U.S. companies such as Intel were hit by falling prices spurred by aggressive Japanese price cutting in 1985 and 1986. The U.S. Department of Commerce supported the dumping claims and has sent them to the International Trade Commission. It may be difficult for U.S. companies to substantiate this claim, however. Recent evidence shows that silicon chip prices in Japan are actually lower than they are in the United States.

While it is possible that businesses have engaged, and will continue to engage, in some sort of cutthroat competition, we do have to assume that businesses ultimately only engage in such acts in order to make higher profits. That means that the future flow of increased profits (properly **discounted** back to today's prices) must somehow exceed the present size of the losses incurred during the pricing war when the predator is pricing below marginal cost. Suffice it to say that there are not too many examples of situations where this has proved to be the case.

SUMMARY

The harsh terms *cutthroat pricing* and *predatory pricing* both refer to a technique used by aggressive business firms wishing to obtain a monopoly in the marketplace. Predatory pricing involves selling at a loss, presumably selling below marginal cost, in order to cause competitors to lose profits until they are forced to leave the marketplace. U.S. antitrust law was created to prohibit this type and other types of monopolizing practices. In recent years, lawsuits have been brought against Japanese firms alleging that such firms are violating antitrust laws by undercutting American prices and dumping their goods in this country. In the recently decided Supreme Court case brought by Zenith Corporation against Japanese television makers, the Supreme Court ruled for the Japanese and clearly warned American businesses not to use antitrust laws to discourage competition. *Dumping* in a term used to describe a situation where producers sell products at high prices domestically to subsidize low-cost sales abroad until a share of the foreign market is obtained. The Japanese have been accused of dumping products in the United States. Even if this were the case, however—and such a claim would be difficult to substantiate—American consumers would benefit by the lower prices, or so at least say proponents of dumping.

DISCUSSION QUESTIONS

1. Do you believe that free access to American markets by Japanese electronic firms is good for the American consumer in the short run? In the long run?
2. Do you agree with the Justices' ruling in the *Zenith* case?
3. Do you feel that the dumping (if it exists) of Japanese products in the United States is harmful or beneficial to Americans?

part three

Factor Markets

INTRODUCTION

Supply and demand analysis also applies to the market for factors of production. These factors of production may be in the form of **labor** or **capital**. Most of the chapters in this part deal with the factor we call *labor*. In Chapter 14, we analyze the issue of comparable worth, whose advocates allege that female labor is obtained at a below-market wage because of sex discrimination. The effect of labor-market opportunities for women on the divorce rate is then explored in Chapter 15.

In Chapter 16, whose subject is professional sports, we analyze labor market restrictions in which the purchasers of the labor input band together to form a monopoly. This type of monopoly is called a **monopsony**—single buyer. An effective monopsony can reduce the wage rate obtained by the individuals affected, and that is indeed what has occurred off and on in professional sports. Chapter 17 analyzes the effect of rent controls on the supply of housing in New York, and Chapter 18 looks at the use of labor and capital by the police as if police personnel were attempting to minimize their costs for any given output. The output is crime prevention and the inputs are labor and capital. Finally, in Chapter 19 the effect of higher taxes on the labor supply is discussed.

Again, we caution the reader that we are not analyzing individuals' thought processes, but rather their observed behavior patterns and the way those behavior patterns change according to the changing constraints.

14

the economics of
Comparable Worth

The Lord spoke to Moses saying: Speak to the Israelite people and say to them: When a man explicitly vows to the Lord the equivalent for a human being, the following scales shall apply: If it is a male from 20 to 60 years of age, the equivalent is 50 shekels of silver by the sanctuary weight; if it is a female, the equivalent is 30 shekels.

—Leviticus, 27:1–4

The Lord in the time of Moses, according to the Five Books of Moses, valued women at 60 percent of the going rate for men. In the job market of today, things haven't changed much. On average, women are paid 65 cents for every dollar paid to men. And 80 percent of the women in the work force are clustered in a heap at the bottom of the pay scale in jobs that have traditionally been dominated by women. Numerous groups, particularly those run by and affecting women, have attempted to alter the situation by legislation. Indeed, a bill to establish greater pay equity among male and female federal employees was passed by the House in 1984 but died in the Senate.

The argument for *equitable* pay goes much further than the *equal* pay requirements mandated by the Equal Pay Act of 1963. That act required employers to pay males and females equal wages if they held the same type of positions. The proponents of pay equity, however, aren't talking about equal pay for males and females holding the *same* job, but equal pay for males and females holding different jobs that are of *comparable worth* to the employer. Under attack is the wage differential between jobs typically held by women (clerical and secretarial positions, for example) and those held by men (such as maintenance jobs).

But, as some critics of the comparable-worth notion maintain, isn't this like comparing apples and oranges? Is it possible to measure the "worth" of widely disparate jobs? Yes, say pay-equity committees across the nation. This can be done by assigning "points" to various job classifications on the basis of job characteristics. Such characteristics include the level of educational training and skills required to perform a job, as well as the responsibilities, mental demands, and working conditions associated with the position. In Minnesota, for example, a registered nurse and a vocational educational teacher are each assigned 275 points, whereas a typing-pool supervisor is assigned 199 points and a painter 185 points. (It must be pointed out, though, that the actual salaries in Minnesota do not yet correspond to this point system.) The higher the points assigned to a job classification, the higher the "worth" of the job to the employer. And, if a "pink-collar" job is associated with the same number of points as a "blue-collar" job, the employees holding those positions should be paid the same wage rate.

The idea of comparable worth grew out of the civil rights legislation of the 1960s. Advocates of comparable worth specifically justify their claims on the basis of Title VII of the Civil Rights Act of 1964, which prohibits wage discrimination on the basis of race, sex, religion, or national origin. In order to link their cause more firmly to both federal and state antidiscrimination laws, supporters of pay equity among male- and female-dominated jobs in the marketplace have abandoned the term *comparable worth* in favor of *sex-based wage discrimination* when discussing the issue. The latter description more effectively links existing wage disparities to sex bias, which is at the heart of the issue.

On the whole, the courts have been sympathetic to the many lawsuits brought, especially by the American Federation of State, County, and Municipal Employees (AFSCME). In 1983, that union won a court decision in Washington state upholding the comparable-worth doctrine. Even though in 1985 a three-judge (all-male) Federal Appeals Court panel in San Francisco overturned the Washington decision, the Washington state legislature had appropriated $482 million to settle the pay dispute. The AFSCME has won about $140 million in settlements in California, Iowa, Wisconsin, Minnesota, New York, and Connecticut.

Critics of comparable worth still abound, however, and the arguments against equitable pay take a variety of forms. On the one hand are those who dismiss the idea as an insensible demand by women for preferential treatment. Such, for example, was the opinion voiced in 1984 by Clarence Pendleton, chairperson of the U.S. Civil Rights Commission, who also called comparable worth "the looniest idea since 'Looney Tunes.' " On the other hand, there are those who argue against the idea on economic grounds. In the latter camp are economists and individuals who stress that the market forces of supply and demand should determine wage rates—not government legislation.

A particular target for criticism is the assumption that jobs can be evaluated objectively and the relative worth or value of jobs classified by numbers in a point system. Economist Richard E. Burr of Washington University, after comparing comparable-worth job evaluations in three states, found wide variation in the "worth" of different jobs among the states. He noted, for example, that a Minnesota librarian is worth 30 percent more than a Vermont librarian who in turn is worth 20 percent more than one in Iowa. Many other job classifications had similar wide variances in value. He also noted substantial variation among states in the criteria used to evaluate the value of jobs. And even within one state, job evaluators had trouble agreeing upon point assignments for job classifications. He cited the case of New Mexico, where, he maintained, four of eight job evaluators agreed on the worth of only 8 percent of jobs analyzed. Put another way, half of the evaluators could not agree on the value of a given job in 824 of 896 classifications.[1]

Market mechanisms, contend Burr and other critics, are a far better method of wage determination than the arbitrary point system devised by pay-equity committees. In the marketplace, a job's value is determined by what people are willing to pay. If men earn more than women, then it is because the free-enterprise system places a higher value on their services.

Many reasons have been offered by critics of comparable worth to explain why men are valued higher than women in the wage market. First, it is argued that female workers often leave the labor force during childbearing years. This career interruption creates a lower lifetime income for women because income is closely related to experience—and maternity leaves keep women from acquiring as much experience as men. An additional factor contributing to the lower earnings of women is that women work fewer hours on average than men do. When adjustments are made for differences in hours worked, the median income of women increases slightly relative to that of men. Finally, women have less geographic mobility than men. They will

[1]"The Capriciousness of Comparable Worth," *Minneapolis Star and Tribune*, October 12, 1986, p. 33A.

often choose or be forced to forgo alternative job offers that are attractive because of the geographical choice of their husbands. One researcher, Robert H. Frank of Cornell University, contends that as much as 23 percent of the wage differential between men and women can be accounted for by such geographic immobility.[2]

Advocates of comparable worth—or pay equity—respond to these arguments by maintaining that, in the first place, wage determination shouldn't be left to the marketplace as that would only perpetuate the sex-based discrimination prohibited by civil rights legislation. They would readily agree with the statement made by Ray Marshall, former Secretary of Labor under President Carter, that "when Adam Smith's invisible hand moves in the labor market, it's all thumbs." Nurses have learned, for example, that market forces such as a nursing shortage don't result in higher pay for individual nurses. Proponents of the comparable worth doctrine also contend that corporate benefits, such as extended, paid-for maternity leaves and on-site daycare centers, have done much to make women as good a "risk" as men in the work arena in terms of long-term employment. And, finally, the argument that women are less mobile than men is countered by the assertion that, if women were paid equally to men, they would have much greater choice when it comes to job mobility.

Among the proponents of comparable worth are some economists who believe that a comparable-worth policy would benefit the economy overall. Mark Aldrich and Robert Buchele, for example, believe that pay discrimination against workers in female-dominated jobs reduces those female workers' wages by about 10–15 percent. They believe that a pay adjustment that raises the wages of workers in female-dominated jobs by a similar amount would help to create a

[2]Robert H. Frank, "Why Women Earn Less: The Theory and Estimates of Differential Overqualification," *American Economic Review*, June 1978, pp. 360–373.

more efficient and less discriminating labor markets. According to these economists, such a wage increase would represent a redress for job segregation rather than "an unwarranted intervention in efficient labor markets."[3] They contend that, in any event, job evaluation in the private sector as it is presently practiced is "profoundly arbitrary."

Although to date the courts have been left to decide the issue, ultimately enough support may be gathered for the cause of comparable worth to induce Congress to legislate pay-equity laws. Several states, apart from those mentioned above, have already implemented plans to equalize pay in male- and female-dominated job classifications, and many labor associations and unions, including the AFL-CIO, have endorsed comparable worth. Also, a small but growing number of employers are already establishing pay-equity scales in a straightforward attempt to update their personnel practices.

It is not the purpose of this chapter either to promote or to criticize the doctrine of comparable worth. Rather, we have sought to analyze the pros and cons of this movement from an analytical, economic point of view. It is hard to escape the conclusion, however, that at heart the issue is more profoundly political than economic, and that moral and political—rather than economic—convictions probably will determine the outcome of this controversial issue.

SUMMARY

Women today earn, on average, approximately 65 percent of what men earn. Many attribute this wage disparity to discrimination against women in the workplace and maintain that such discrimination violates Title VII of the Civil Rights Act of 1964. It is argued that comparable-worth laws—mandating comparable pay for jobs of comparable value to em-

[3]The Economics of Comparable Worth (Cambridge, MA: Ballinger Publishing Co., 1986), p. 174.

ployers—should be enacted to prevent such discrimination. Comparable worth does not mean that men and women holding the same type of job should receive equal pay, but that men and women holding different jobs should receive equal pay if they are of "comparable worth" to the employer. Critics of comparable worth maintain that such a doctrine ignores the economic forces at work in the marketplace, particularly the laws of supply and demand as they relate to labor. These opponents feel that the marketplace, not the government, should determine wage rates, and that so far the marketplace has deemed women less valuable than men for valid economic reasons. To date, the comparable-worth issue has failed to gain the full support of Congress and has thus been decided mainly by the courts, which have tried a host of lawsuits concerning the issue. On the whole, the courts have looked favorably upon the issue of comparable worth, and several states have implemented plans to equalize pay for male- and female-dominated job classifications.

DISCUSSION QUESTIONS

1. Do you think that comparable-worth laws would represent preferential treatment for women? Why or why not?
2. When the Federal Appeals Court in San Francisco overturned the State of Washington federal court decision in 1985, the panel of judges ruled that the state was under no obligation "to eliminate an economic inequality which it did not create." Do you agree with this opinion?

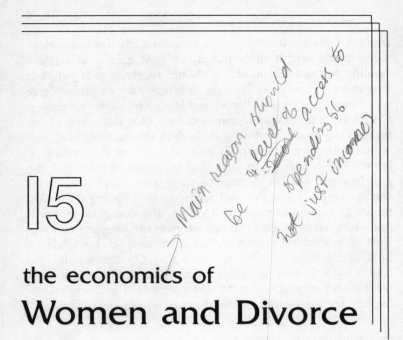

(handwritten marginalia) Main reason should be the level of access to ~~their~~ spending $ not just income (earnings)

15

the economics of
Women and Divorce

Today, about 6 million women are making more income than their mates. And another 2½ million women are earning at least 80 percent of the pay of their husbands.

What kind of women outstrip their husbands in their earning capacity? The Census Bureau reports that wives with higher wages are most likely to be working full time, year round, with no minor children at home. Also, they usually have completed college and are employed in a professional, administrative, executive, or managerial occupation.

What does the fact that some women are making almost as much as, or more than, their husbands have to do with the title of this chapter? As it turns out, economic theory predicts that divorce rates will be influenced by, among other things, the earning capacity of women. In the most general sense, the more that a married woman can earn on

TABLE 15-1 Percent of Men and Women Ever Married Who Were Known to Have Been Divorced, by Place of Residence (1970 Data)

	Divorce Rates	
Location	Male	Female
Urban	14.6	15.5
Rural nonfarm	13.1	12.0
Rural farm	7.4	6.6

Source: U.S. Department of Commerce, *Statistical Abstract of the United States 1980*, U.S. Government Printing Office, Washington, D. C.

her own, the less she has to give up if she chooses to become divorced. In other words, the opportunity cost of divorce is less for women with higher earning potential.

We can apply this theory to information gleaned about divorce rates of rural versus urban females. Look at Table l5-1. As you can see, rural farm men and women have substantially lower divorce rates than either rural nonfarm (small-town) men and women or urban men and women. A sociological or psychological explanation of these data might be that life is happier for men and women on the farm than it is for urban couples. It is indeed possible that this is true. Economists, however, look for explanations based on the choices available to individuals and the relative costs and benefits attached to these choices. That is to say, when looking for explanations of real-world phenomena, economists will tend to look at opportunity costs and trade-offs and interpret events in these terms.

Department of Labor statistics tell us that about 50 percent of nonfarm women are in the labor force, but only about 30 percent of farm women are employed (off the farm). In other words, farm women tend to specialize more in household and on-farm work relative to nonfarm women. Men on farms maintain a specialization in nonhousehold work. The gains to marriage are therefore greater in a farming household, on average, than in a nonfarming household. Essentially, then, we would predict that farm households would be more stable than nonfarm households. Moreover, we would predict that the opportunity cost for the farm wife who has specialized in household and on-farm work would be greater in a divorce than the opportunity cost of a non-farm wife who is employed in a nonfarm job. That is because the nonfarm wife will give up less by becoming divorced because she already has an earning capacity.

Take another look at Table 15-1. You will note that the divorce rate for women living on farms is lower than for men living on farms. But the opposite is true in urban areas, where females have a higher divorce rate than males. How can we explain this? Economic theory assumes that individuals desire to maximize their net benefits and that in order to maximize net benefits, they will seek out their best opportunities. That is to say, they will tend to migrate to wherever the best opportunities exist. When a farm marriage ends in divorce, the male typically retains farm ownership; he stays on the farm to work. The female, on the other hand, moves to where her job opportunities will be greater—to urban areas.

Census data reveal that divorce rates for farm women are higher among women who live on farms located in areas with relatively dense populations, such as in Massachusetts and New Jersey. Can economic theory also help us to understand why this would be the case? As it turns out, yes. Farm women living in those areas, because of their closer proximity to urban labor markets, have a better knowledge of other labor opportunities. That means that in those areas the opportunity cost to women on farms of learning about alternative uses of their labor is less. Also, in such relatively densely populated areas it is much easier to work at nonfarm jobs—which means, among other things, that they have less incentive to invest in farm-specific skills only. By contrast, farm women living in the sparsely populated states of Nevada and Wyoming, for example, have not had similar opportunities to become aware of job alternatives off the farm or to learn nonfarm-specific skills. Therefore, they have tended to specialize more in farm-specific skills and household skills. We would predict, therefore, that the differences between farm and nonfarm divorce rates is lowest in the most densely populated states and highest in the most sparsely populated states. Indeed, the data show that this prediction is accurate.

Increasing numbers of nonfarm women are entering the work force each year. In the wake of the current agricultural crisis, many farm women, along with their families, are being forced to leave the business of farming and also are entering the nonfarm labor market. And, slowly but surely, wages for women are rising relative to wages of men. Does this mean that the divorce rate will increase in the future? If the assumptions in this chapter are correct, then we can predict that it will. In general, the greater the number of opportunities available to an individual, and the lower the cost of those opportunities, the more likely it is that they will be explored—and sometimes this entails a divorce.

SUMMARY

Economic theory predicts that divorce rates will be influenced by the earning capacity of women. This is because the opportunity cost of divorce is less for women who can earn income outside the home. This theory is borne out by the fact that divorce rates are higher among nonfarm women (50 percent of whom are employed) than among farm women (30 percent of whom are employed in nonfarm labor). Divorce rates among farm women are also higher in relatively densely populated areas than in sparsely populated areas. This is because farm women in the more densely populated areas have more opportunities to learn of job alternatives and are closer to the nonfarm labor market than is the case in the sparsely populated areas of the country. In general, the greater the number of opportunities available to an in-

dividual and the lower the cost of those opportunities, the
more likely it is that they will be explored.

DISCUSSION QUESTIONS

1. On the basis of the analysis given in this chapter,
   would you assume divorce rates would be highest
   among women who have the highest incomes?
2. To what extent do you think opportunities and opportunity costs are determining factors in divorce
   decisions?

16

the economics of
Professional Sports

use Monopsony model

Professional sports have held a unique position in American life. They have also held a somewhat unique position in the eyes of the American court system. Because of the latter, owners of professional sports teams and leagues have been able to engage in monopolizing practices that are forbidden to other American businesses. Thus, monopolies over the labor markets for baseball, football, and basketball have, by and large, gone unchallenged by the courts. How are such monopolies accomplished? One monopolizing tactic that was successfully used for many years was the "reserve clause," a clause in a player's contract that gave the team exclusive rights to the player's services until he was sold, traded, or released by the team.

To understand the effect of such reserve clauses on the labor markets for baseball, basketball, and football, we will

first look at a labor market which has no reserve clause—
the labor market for gardeners. Most gardeners charge what
they think is the "going" price for their services. If one
charges considerably less than this price, some potential additional customers will eventually find out. He will then find
himself with many new requests for his services. If he is not
willing to put extra hours into gardening, he will have to
decide on one, or a combination, of the following courses:
(1) lowering the quality of his service so that each job requires less time, and thus squeeze in more customers; (2)
refusing the additional work; or (3) raising his prices so that
certain customers, present or potential, will not be interested
in obtaining his services. Obviously, the first choice is equivalent to the third, since a change in quality at the same price
exerts the same economic effect as a change in price for the
same quality.

On the other hand, a gardener who does not have
enough work and wishes to attract more customers is free
to lower his price or raise the quality of his services. That
is, gardeners can compete among themselves to maximize
their own individual incomes. To be sure, not all gardeners
do this.

Now let's assume that a particular gardener gains a reputation for doing exceptionally good work. If he already has
a full schedule, a potential customer will have to offer some
incentive to gain his services on a regular basis. An adequate
incentive might persuade the gardener to do one of the following: (1) work more intensively, (2) work longer hours and
take fewer holidays, or (3) drop one of his former customers.

The usual form of incentive is an offer of higher wages,
although incentives are not always monetary. In any case,
by employing such tactics, people desiring to obtain gardeners' services are competing among themselves. Although
not all homeowners take the trouble to find out which gardener in the neighborhood gives the best service at the lowest price, some do.

We have just described the workings of a competitive

market in gardening. Gardeners are free to vary the price, quantity, and quality of the service they sell. Homeowners are free to vary the price (wage) they offer and the quantity and quality of service they demand. Theoretically, gardeners end up getting a wage that just equals the value of their services (i.e., they are paid the value of their marginal product). Buyers of gardeners' services end up paying for the opportunity cost of these services, no more, no less (i.e., they must pay the value of the gardeners' marginal product).

What would happen if all homeowners in the country got together and decided to institute a "gardening reserve clause"? The clause would require that each individual gardener work for only one homeowner (or, more realistically in this case, for one group of owners). The gardener could not work anywhere else unless the owner of the contract with the reserve clause decided that he, the owner, wanted to sell or trade the contract. Notice that one crucial aspect of the previously described competitive market has been eliminated: Gardeners cannot seek out the most advantageous job opportunities or compete for business, because only the homeowners can initiate a move. It is surely apparent that such restraint would prevent gardeners from seeking employment that would maximize their income and that it could leave them worse off than they were under free and competitive conditions.

They not only could, but most certainly *would*, be worse off if all homeowners then got together to form a cartel with the express agreement that they would not compete among themselves for gardeners' contracts. Competition in the gardening market would be stifled on both sides: among the sellers of gardening services and among the buyers of those services.[1]

---

[1]Of course it is hard to imagine that a cartel of so many people would actually work. The incentive to cheat would be too great, the problem of inducing new homeowners to join would be large, and the cost of enforcement of the agreement would be tremendous.

What is pure hypothesis in our example was reality in the world of baseball for many years. The major league teams had made agreements among themselves that yielded a very special players' contract. Since the terms included an agreement not to tamper with a player "reserved" by any team, the contracting club, in effect, held a unilateral option on the player's services for the following year. Once the player signed, he accepted all agreements made between teams; therefore, his only course was to attempt to get the highest possible salary from his particular team, with no help from competing teams. The player's choice was simple: to accept the offered salary or not to play baseball—at least not with any U.S. major league team.

The reserve clause allowed a baseball team to restrain the workings of the job market for baseball players. Therefore, a monopoly element entered into baseball hirings.[2] Baseball teams contended that the reserve clause was essential to the game because it allowed for an even distribution of good players among all teams. It was asserted that without the reserve rules, richer clubs would bid away the best talent. Games would be lopsided, and bored spectators would quit buying tickets.

Although plausible at first glance, this argument loses validity when one realizes that any industry could make a similar statement. In practice, rich firms do not buy up all the best workers and thus make the manufacturing "game" lopsided. Firms and baseball clubs can always borrow money to invest in good workers and good players if the potential payoff for doing so is high enough. Obviously, if only one good (rich) team existed, the payoff from building a competing good team would be high enough to allow a club to borrow money (or sell additional stock) to do so.

Moreover, the value of players depends on gate receipts. How large would ticket sales be with only one good team? Few people would want to see a slaughter at every

[2]The technically correct term is *monopsonist*—one buyer.

game involving the best, richest team. Therefore, it behooves good teams to ensure that there are other good teams to compete against in order to generate suspense, excitement, and the resulting higher gate receipts.

The reserve clause was an attempt to restrict competition among teams for players. As a result, players were making less money than they would have without the clause. Also as a result of this clause, many players brought antitrust suits against professional baseball league owners. Antitrust legislation, beginning with the Sherman Antitrust Act of 1890, specifically prohibits American businesses from engaging in actions that are in restraint of trade and commerce; in other words, monopolies and monopolizing practices are forbidden. But baseball was exempted from such legislation in a Supreme Court ruling in 1922, because baseball was not considered to be "commerce" in the sense stipulated by the Sherman Act. This exemption was upheld in a 1953 ruling and again in 1972, when Curt Flood lost an antitrust case against baseball league owners.

The impact of the reserve clause on players' salaries was, for quite some time, augmented by the effects of a compact between the National and American leagues *not* to compete for each other's players. Such an arrangement would suggest the potential for a third league to bid the best players away from the other two by offering higher salaries. No third U.S. league could have succeeded, however, because players who might have signed with it would be forever barred from the American and National leagues. Apparently not enough players were willing to take this chance, and no other major league appeared.

In an attempt to counter the monopoly power of the baseball team owners, a baseball players' **union** was formed. The union was ultimately successful in its attempts to secure higher salaries for the players and to improve their pension plans. It also succeeded eventually in removing the reserve clause from the players' contracts.

At least up until 1986 (at the writing of this edition),

professional football was an almost exact image of what professional baseball used to be. The National Football League (NFL) was the only league in existence from 1919 until 1960, when the American Football League (AFL) appeared. With the appearance of the AFL, players' salaries promptly increased manyfold.

When the NFL ruled the scene, teams could "draft" players and effectively keep them as long as they wanted. No competition by larger salary offers was allowed. A collusive agreement among NFL team owners prevented players from maximizing their incomes, and no competing league existed to bid players away.

The NFL draft system, which began in 1936, prohibits a college player from negotiating with any professional team other than the one that drafts him. Generally, the worst teams in the league are allowed the first draft choices, presumably to give them a better chance in the forthcoming season.

More than a decade ago, the Washington Redskins drafted star defensive back Jim (Yazoo) Smith. His record at the University of Oregon was impressive, and as a rookie he was good enough to make the starting lineup for the Redskins. Unfortunately, in the the final game of the season, Smith suffered a severe neck injury that ended his career. In September 1976, U.S. Judge William B. Bryant awarded Smith $276,000 in damages—not because of his physical injuries, but because he suffered financial losses. Smith had contended that the league's draft system had restricted his bargaining power with the Redskins, and that the negotiations were so lopsided that he was prevented from obtaining a contract that would have given him financial security when and if he suffered a disabling injury. When the judge struck down the NFL's annual draft of college players, he commented that "this outright, undisguised refusal to deal constitutes a group boycott in its classic and most pernicious form, a device which has long been condemned as per se violation of the antitrust laws." Bryant further added that the draft procedure was "absolutely the most restrictive one imaginable." He also suggested some changes the NFL might make to satisfy the court. For example, three teams might be allowed to choose one player and then bid for that player's services. This, of course, would improve the bargaining position of the players.[3]

In 1966, after six years of "competition," the AFL and NFL agreed to merge. Congress approved the move as a rider to a public housing bill![4] This merger has affected the freedom of players. Although the terms state that after playing out his contract's one-year option a player may sign with another team, if he does so, the second team must compensate the original team. This, of course, discourages recruitment by the second team. The player can also attempt to arrange a trade through the offices of the football commissioner; however, to date, the results of such negotiations have not been very favorable to the players involved. By precluding the need to compete for players, the AFL-NFL merger has clearly held the salaries of players lower than they would have been under freely competitive conditions.

Unlike baseball, professional football is not exempt from antitrust laws. Nonetheless, the NFL has succeeded in weathering the competitive challenges posed by the American Football League in the 1960s, the World Football League in the 1970s, and the United States Football League (USFL) in the 1980s.

For a short time in 1986, however, the NFL monopoly in the area of professional football was seriously threatened by a $1.7-billion antitrust suit brought against the NFL by the three-year-old USFL. In the court battle that took place to decide the issue, the USFL alleged that the NFL had con-

[3]Note that if no reserve clause existed, the draft system would not work because it would not allocate property rights; without the reserve clause the team owners do not obtain property rights in the players' contracts.
[4]This in spite of a 1967 court ruling that football was subject to antitrust laws.

spired to pressure the major television networks into refusing to air USFL games. If this continued, it would result in the end of the fledgling league, because the sale of television rights was crucial to the USFL's potential income. The USFL also claimed that the NFL had tried to sabotage its franchises in large cities such as New York. The NFL, in return, denied these allegations and accused the USFL of suing in order to bring about a merger. It also maintained that the USFL's numerous financial troubles, which included the bankruptcy of many of its franchises, was a result of poor management and lack of public interest, not NFL duplicity.

The USFL brought forth many star witnesses and much evidence to support its claims. One of the witnesses was former broadcaster Howard Cosell, who, according to Chuck Sullivan (vice president of the NFL's New England Patriots), had admitted to Sullivan privately that the NFL was making "overtly antitrust" actions. Al Davis, owner of the Los Angeles Raiders, testified that the NFL tried to weaken the USFL's Oakland Outlaws in order to clear the Oakland area for a possible NFL team.

The court's decision clearly affirmed that the NFL holds a unique status in the eyes of the law. The jury decided, on the one hand, that the NFL is indeed a monopoly. On the other, however, it ruled that the NFL was not responsible for the USFL's decline. The $1 awarded in damages to the USFL symbolized its agonizing victory, and it was hardly enough to compensate for the $70 million annual losses the USFL had suffered during its short existence. A few days later, the USFL announced that there would be no 1986 season.

This decision, in effect, took away the bargaining power of professional football players. Without the rival league, the players have no alternative but either to accept the contracts offered to them or not to play football. Although free agency has existed in the NFL since 1977, it is very rarely used. In fact, only one player, little-known Norm Johnson, has ever changed teams via free agency. In 1985, Walter Payton, one of the great players in the history of the sport, applied for free agency but received no bids. The players contend that the reason for this is because the owners are more interested in making a profit than in producing a winning team. And because of the huge money paid uniformly to the owners by television networks, it is not necessary for the owners to spend large amounts of money to procure other teams' players. This issue will certainly be the focus of contract renegotiations when the Players' Association's pact with the NFL runs out in 1987.

SUMMARY

Monopolistic (technically, monopsonistic) practices have existed in the area of professional sports for decades. Owners of professional sports teams and leagues have used reserve clauses and agreements not to compete to create and maintain monopoly power over the labor market in sports. By and large, the courts have not challenged these overt violations of antitrust laws. Baseball was declared exempt from antitrust legislation in 1922, an exemption that has been upheld since in further court decisions. The NFL's virtual monopoly over the professional football market has also not been challenged by the courts, although football is subject to antitrust laws. Even though a court decision in 1986 conceded that the NFL was indeed a monopoly, no action was taken against it and the plaintiff (USFL) was awarded no damages other than the token $1 in this $1.7 billion antitrust suit.

DISCUSSION QUESTIONS

1. What prevents monopolization in the purchase of inputs (a monopsony) from existing in most labor markets?
2. How can you explain the unwillingness by the courts to enforce antitrust legislation in the case of professional football?

17

the economics of
The Big Apple

In this chapter we shall explore some of the ramifications of setting prices below a market-clearing price. We will do this by examining the consequences of rent control in New York City.[1]

First, it will help to describe briefly the way in which a market adjusts to changes in supply and demand, both in the short run and the long run. In this instance, we mean by the short run a period of time too short for the building of new housing units. Now that does not mean that the supply is perfectly inelastic. Why not? Because a higher price for housing will encourage people who own homes or hous-

---

[1]New York is not alone in its rent-control problems. Some 200 cities around the nation, including Los Angeles, Berkeley, San Francisco, and Washington, D.C., also have some form of rent controls that prevent landlords from charging tenants what they choose.

ing units to rent part of their units rather than keep them all for themselves. There is, therefore, some short-run elasticity of supply. A shift in demand, reflecting, as it did in New York during World War II, a sudden increase of people seeking apartments, would lead to a sharp rise in price and some increase in the quantity of units available.

The consequence, in the long run, is to set in motion the forces that make for a new equilibrium, which is essentially the way a market system works. A sharp rise in the price of apartments makes it attractive for entrepreneurs to invest their money in building new housing. To put it another way, the rate of return to investing in the housing stock has increased as compared to other ways an entrepreneur could use his or her capital. This results in new construction, which in turn leads to a downward movement in the price of housing as the supply increases, until ultimately an equilibrium is reached. Note that the implication is that the long-run supply of housing is relatively elastic under free market conditions, in contrast to the short run. The long-run equilibrium is one in which the rate of return on investing in one more unit of housing is just equal to that of investing in any other similar economic activity with the same degree of risk.

Now back to our story of New York. In 1943, the federal government imposed rent control as a temporary wartime measure. While the federal program ended after the war, it was continued in New York State, and specifically in New York City. The law in the city kept rent for certain categories of apartments at fixed levels, allowing an increase in the rental price only when a tenant moved out. Getting a tenant to move out, however, proved to be difficult. In normal circumstances, such turnover could occur whenever a tenant's lease expired. Under New York City laws, however, a landlord had to renew the lease if an existing tenant wanted to continue renting the apartment. Needless to say, an immediate consequence was that landlords tended to encourage such departures by everything from pounding on the pipes to cutting off the heat. Since there were many more people seeking apartments than there were apartments available, a longer-run consequence was the development of a vast array of devices to attempt to get around the restrictions. The most obvious was what was called key money, which was a way to charge a prospective renter a large amount of money simply to get the key to an apartment; or one could hire the landlord's son to repaint the apartment at a substantial fee. In other cases, the landlord would discriminate among prospective tenants on the basis of race, religion, dogs, children, or whatever. Still another consequence was that landlords simply failed to maintain apartments, so their real costs of upkeep were decreased.

One obvious consequence of rent control was widespread evasion of the law, and, in turn, a multitude of city regulations were created to curb these evasions. Landlords in such a situation have every incentive to be obnoxious and to enforce lease terms as strictly as possible. City authorities have countered with laws protecting tenants and by banning or restricting the enforcement of numerous lease provisions, such as those prohibiting pets or unrelated roommates. Recently, a law has been passed stating that even if a landlord proves in court that a tenant has broken a lease, the tenant, if he or she can demonstrate that the violation has been corrected, cannot be evicted. And if the violation recurs a few days or weeks later, the landlord's only recourse is more legal fees for a repeat performance. The assignment of rights to an existing lease and subletting apartments were also prohibited by the city, but these laws have been widely evaded. In a recent directive, partially aimed at those evading the subletting prohibition, Major Koch stipulated that persons who maintain their tax residence outside of the city forfeit their right to retain rent-controlled apartments.

The tactics resorted to by landlords and tenants in New York suggest that they have simply been finding ways to get around the artificially low price and develop a *de facto* equilibrium. That is, the real value of apartments has fallen and/or the tenant in fact has paid an extra price. Thus, in reality, shifts in the supply and demand curves have occurred.

Nevertheless, rent control has significant consequences for both renter and landlord. Clearly, a landlord suffers in terms of a drop in income and a renter suffers in terms of a quality reduction in apartments. However, that is not the end of the story. As of 1986, of the 650,000 apartment units in the borough of Manhattan alone, roughly 420,000 were subject to rent restrictions. During the whole period since World War II, there has been almost no construction of apartments that would be subject to rent control. Moreover, apartments deteriorated because it was not worthwhile for landlords to keep them up; eventually the annual taxes on the apartment houses exceeded the income the landlord received, and the apartments were simply abandoned. In the 1970s, approximately 40,000 units were abandoned. In some parts of the Bronx and on Manhattan's lower East Side, whole rows of abandoned apartment houses stood gutted and stripped by vandals. After a certain interval, the city takes over such buildings for back taxes. By 1984, the city had acquired more than 120,000 units in this way. Unlike other areas, though, in New York properties claimed for back taxes do not get auctioned off to new owners. Rather, they become a part of the city's public-housing stock. The cost to the city is, as you might expect, enormous. Currently, the city pays more than $150 million a year for its housing-reclamation program.

It is unlikely that rent controls will be lifted in New York in the near future. Indeed, it appears that the opposite will be the case. Housing activists are pressing for controls over buildings that have been, to date, exempt, such as buildings with fewer than six units, some housing units owned by nonprofit organizations, and commercial property.

The long-run consequences of rent controls in New York City have been a decay in the housing stock and a decline in the amount of available space for middle- and lower-income tenants (luxury apartments, exempted from rent control, have continued to be built). In spite of these consequences, however, and notwithstanding the budget crises that have faced the city in past years, sentiment supporting rent control in the Big Apple is as strong as ever.

SUMMARY

Each production activity requires factors of production. Use of those factors of production will continue as long as at least a normal rate of return can be obtained. The provision of housing services is no different than the provision of any other product or service—it requires factors of production. Rent controls restrict the ability of landlords to charge a market-clearing price. To the extent that rent controls are effective, they can lead to a reduction in the current quality of housing services available as well as a reduction in the future supply of housing services. Investors who cannot make a normal rate of return will no longer choose to invest in apartment buildings. Therefore, rent controls can have a short-run effect and a long-run effect. Both effects have a negative impact on many individuals seeking "affordable" housing.

DISCUSSION QUESTIONS

1. Who benefits from rent controls in the short run? In the long run?
2. Why would any landlord ever completely abandon an apartment building?

18

the economics of
Crime Prevention

In 1986, New York City appropriated $1,321,120,415 for the police department for the following year. We start our examination with an assumption that the amount of resources devoted to crime prevention is inversely related to the amount of crime. Had the city of New York appropriated twice that amount, would there be less crime? How much less? In short, what is the relation between prevention of crime and money spent? How did the city decide on that figure?

Before we can begin to answer these questions, we must look in greater detail at the economics of fighting crime. First of all, it is not just the police and other law-enforcement agencies that are involved in crime prevention. The courts and various types of penal and reform institu-

113

tions also enter the picture, as do devices such as burglar alarms, locks, and safes.

Law enforcement has many aspects and the costs of each must be considered in allocating the resources available. The costs can be divided into three general areas. First there are the costs of the crime detection (in cases such as narcotics or prostitution) and the arrest of suspects. Second, costs are involved in the trial and conviction of the prisoner; they vary with the efficiency and speed with which the law-enforcement officials and the courts can act. Third, once sentence is imposed, there are the economic costs of maintaining and staffing prisons. This third area and the social implications of the queston of what sorts and durations of punishment are most effective as deterrents to crime will be examined in Chapter 25.

As noted above, the amount of resources devoted to discovering and apprehending criminals is related to a reduction in crime. But the optimum allocation of those resources is not so clear-cut. The chief of police or the commissioner is faced with two sets of problems. On the one hand, this individual must decide how to divide the funds between capital and labor—that is, choose between more cars, equipment, and laboratories or more police personnel, detectives, and technicians. On the other hand, he or she must also allocate funds among the various police details within the department—for example, deciding whether to clamp down harder on homicide or on car theft or on drug traffic.

Within a law-enforcement budget of a given size, the police chief must then determine the optimum combination of production factors. The ideal combination is one in which an additional dollar spent on any one of the labor or capital inputs will provide an equal additional amount of enforcement. If an additional dollar spent on laboratory equipment yields a higher crime-deterrent result than the same dollar spent on a police officer's salary, the laboratory will win. While it is clear that inputs cannot be measured in such small amounts, the question of *indivisibility*,[1] or lumpiness in production, does not alter the basic argument. Nor does it alter the argument that we cannot precisely measure the returns on an increase in labor or in some input of capital. The police captain must normally judge from experience and intuition as well as from available data whether buying more cars or hiring more men and women will do the better job in checking crime. And note that this decision may change with changes in relative price. For example, when the salaries of police officers are raised, the balance may tip toward the use of more cars or equipment, depending on how well captial can be substituted for labor in a given situation. Instead of using two police officers in a car, it might be economically efficient to equip the car with bulletproof glass and let the driver patrol alone.

The second task of the police chief is to determine how to allocate resources among the interdepartmental details. Sometimes highly publicized events may influence this decision. For example, several years ago, prostitution increased in downtown Seattle to such a degree that local merchants protested vigorously that streetwalkers were hurting business. They had sufficient political influence to induce the police chief to step up sharply the detection and apprehension of prostitutes. That meant using more personnel and equipment on the vice squad; and within the restriction of a fixed budget this could be done only by pulling resources away from homicide, robbery, and other details, which were thus made short-handed. In effect, the cost of reducing prostitution was a short-run increase in assault and robbery. It is not clear (in the short run, at least) that political pressure of the sort just mentioned leads to a concentration of police

[1]A good or service is said to be indivisible if it can be sold only in relatively large quantities. For example, one cannot purchase one-tenth of a police car. However, perhaps the car can be rented for one-tenth of each month. Given the possibility of rental, many products can no longer be called indivisible.

enforcement in those areas that many people feel are most essential.

We said that three general areas of law enforcement entail costs to society, and we have just dealt with the area of detection and arrest. The second area is the trial and its outcome. Recent studies indicate that the likelihood of conviction is a highly important factor (if not the major one) in the prevention of crime. Currently, the probability of conviction and punishment for crime is extremely low in the United States. In New York City, it has been estimated that an individual who commits a felony faces less than 1 chance in 200 of going to jail. Poor crime detection partly explains this incredible figure; court congestion adds to the problem. In highly urbanized environments, the court calendar is so clogged that the delay in getting a case to trial may stretch from months into years.[2] One consequence of this situation is an increasing tendency for the prosecutor and suspect to arrange a pretrial settlement rather than further overburden the courts. This is what happens to 80–90 percent of criminal charges. The effect on the morale of the police officers who have brought the cases to trial is obvious. Society may be underinvesting in the resources necessary to improve this process. If more were to be spent on streamlining court proceedings instead of on making arrests, cases could be brought to trial more promptly, the presence of all witnesses could be more easily secured, and the hand of the D.A. would not be forced in making "deals" with suspects. Faced with the probability of quick and efficient trial, a potential criminal might think harder about robbing a bank or mugging a pedestrian. Former Chief Justice Warren E. Burger himself declared that we do in fact need an overhauling of our courts.

There remains another issue, which is highly contro-

---

[2]Many court calendars are solidly booked for two, three, or even five years into the future. In New York, for example, the average time lapse between filing a civil suit and getting it to trial is 39 months.

versial. The likelihood of detection and conviction can be increased by new technical means, by wiretapping, and by changes in the laws protecting the rights of suspects (e.g., permitting law officers to enter and search without knocking, lifting the requirement that suspects be informed of their constitutional rights, and allowing the holding of suspects incommunicado for lengthy periods). However, the consequences of such legal changes in terms of infringement on individual liberties are extremely serious, and in any event we do not have the information necessary to determine how effective such changes would be.

We can now return to our original question. How did New York City determine that a budget for crime prevention of $1,321,120,415 was the right amount? In the short run, the city was faced with a total budget of a given size and had to decide how to carve it up between law enforcement and other municipal demands, such as fire protection, health, parks, streets, and libraries. Just as a police chief may try to determine what combination of police officers and equipment within his or her fixed budget will deter the greatest amount of crime, a city council will attempt to choose a combination of spending on all agencies that will yield the maximum amount of public services. If additional money spent on fire protection does not yield as much "good" as it would if spent on police protection, then the amount should be allocated to law enforcement.[3] Determining the value of services rendered by each agency poses a touchy problem. However, the problem is not insuperable, at least in principle. Crude approximations can be made of the benefits and costs of crime prevention, and the efficiency of the public sector of our economy will be improved as such calculations are made and refined.

The short-run constraint of a fixed budget for law enforcement may be altered in the long run by going to the

[3]The city council equates on the margin returns from money spent on all municipal activities.

state legislature and asking for increased funds for crime prevention. The legislature will then have to wrestle with the same allocation problem that engaged the city council. Funds can be increased for a city's budget only by tightening the belt in some other area, such as school expenditures or park development. The same familiar calculations must also be made on the state level: Will spending an additional dollar on higher education yield greater returns for society than the same dollar given to a city council to allocate to crime prevention? The same difficult question arises in measuring the dollar value of nonpriced services resulting from any given state expenditure.

The state does have an option not open to most city councils in most states: It can raise taxes. If it chooses to, this will widen the allocation problem. The increased taxes will reduce the disposable income of some part of the citizenry. Those who pay the additional taxes must in turn decide whether they feel the additional public services made available are worthwhile. For example, is the reduction in crime attributable to an increased expenditure on law enforcement as valuable to them as the goods they could have enjoyed from that increased tax money? If they do not think so, then at the next election they will vote to "throw the rascals out."

The above description indicates that nonmarket solutions to economic problems run basically parallel to market solutions. Although we have focused on crime prevention, the criteria are similar for all types of government decisions and for all levels of government—local, state, and federal.

But certain differences must also be noted between decision making in the private market sector of the economy and in the public nonmarket sector. Problems of measurement are much greater in the latter. How, for example, do we put a price tag on recreation, which is the output of the parks department? And the signals come through much louder and more clearly in market situations, in which changes in private profitability "telegraph" to entrepreneurs what policies will be best.[4] Instead of market signals, makers of public policy receive a confused set of noises generated by opponents and proponents of their decisions. A legislator is in the unenviable position of trying to please as much of the electorate as possible while operating with very incomplete information.

Some cities have tried to use market mechanisms to improve crime prevention. A few years ago, the city of Orange, California, near Los Angeles, started paying its police according to how much crime was reduced. The incentive scheme applied to four categories of crime—burglary, robbery, rape, and auto theft. Under the plan, as first put into effect, if the crime rate in those categories was cut by 3 percent for the first eight months of the year compared with the first eight months in the previous year, the police would get an extra 1-percent raise. If the crime rate fell by 6 percent, the pay increase would be an extra 2 percent. The results have been encouraging. Detectives on their own time produce videotape briefings with leads for patrol officers on specific beats. The whole force developed a campaign to encourage safety precautions in residents' homes. Statistically speaking, the results were even more impressive, for during the first seven months of the program crime in the four categories listed above fell by 17.62 percent. The other crime figures held steady, indicating that the police force was not merely shifting its efforts from one area of crime to another.

On the basic question of the allocation of resources within a police department or within a municipality, there is a way in which such allocation might be altered. In the early 1980s, in many cities and states a person could be beaten up in the streets and left with permanent brain damage but could not sue for injuries. The attacker, if caught, would be jailed—but that did not help the victim, who ended up paying taxes for the prisoner's room and board!

[4]In instances where **externalities** exist, it may be to society's advantage to alter these signals by appropriate measures.

Victims' rights groups have recently made substantial progress, however. The first move toward compensation of victims of crime for their suffering was an initiative passed in California on June 8, 1982. This initiative was widely referred to as a "bill of rights" for crime victims. It required convicts to make restitution to those harmed (it also made other broad changes such as putting limits on bail releases and insanity pleas). Since then, most of the states have established funds to compensate crime victims. And in 1984, Congress passed the Victims of Crime Act, which in 1986 distributed millions of dollars collected from federal criminal penalties and fines to victims' groups around the country.

But for the most part, the compensation is far less than the full cost of the crime. What if a city or a state were obligated for the full cost of a crime committed within its borders? How would that affect the expenditure on crime prevention? One would surmise that unlimited liability on the part of government for crimes against the populace would certainly alter the present allocation of resources between crime prevention and other public endeavors.

This raises the question of what lawyers call "moral hazard." If victims of robberies, for example, were fully compensated by the municipality, there would be less incentive for individuals to protect themselves privately against robberies. The same is true for other crimes. One way to avoid this "moral hazard" is to establish a deductible on the municipality's liability. For example, for home robberies, the municipality might be held responsible for all losses in excess of $500. If this were the case, homeowners still would have an incentive to lock their doors, have watchdogs, and keep lights on at night when they are away.

Another way in which the allocation of crime-prevention resources might be altered is suggested by a current experiment in crime prevention taking place in Newport News, Virginia, a Navy port city with a population of 157,000. The experiment is the brainchild of Sergeant Martin Evans of the Newport News Police Department, who secured $1.2 million from the federal government to try a highly innovative approach to the problem of crime deterrence. The strategy behind the new approach—referred to as "problem-oriented policing"—is basically to deter crime before the fact, rather than punishing it after the fact. At the heart of the program is a "crime-analysis model," a lengthy questionnaire filled out by police officers whenever a crime is committed. Analysis of these reports over time enables the police to predict, with a surprising degree of accuracy, where crimes are likely to be committed. Steps can then be taken to prevent the crime, if possible, by drawing on other public and private resources in the community—health clinics, social workers, attorneys, welfare agencies, and so on. By analyzing the 28 cases of homicide over an 18-month period ending in July 1985, for example, Sergeant Evans found that 50 percent of all the murders committed had involved family members of the victims and that in half of those cases the police had already had complaints of domestic violence. As a result, a new procedure was implemented. Today, police make arrests whenever they witness domestic violence and don't wait for a husband or a wife—or other family member—to swear out a warrant. The arrested party is placed in jail and is only released if the individual agrees to professional counseling. So far, the counseling has seemed to work: For the five years preceding the experiment, the city had averaged 25 murders a year—half of them the result of domestic violence. During the first six months of the new program, however, only four murders were committed, and only one was a domestic case. In all areas of crime—prostitution, robberies, burglaries, and "nuisance" crimes such as petty theft and vandalism—similar prevention techniques have been used successfully.

Traditionally, police have responded to crime and not taken an active preventive role. The Newport News program involves a radical reorientation toward their work on the part of the police officers involved. The results of the experiment to date indicate that perhaps, if more money and resources were allocated to crime prevention before the fact, the overall high cost of crime might be reduced—for victims and taxpayers alike.

Crime costs. So does crime prevention. But the latter has benefits to society that should be weighed when making decisions about law-enforcement methods and expenditures.

SUMMARY

If we consider crime prevention the output of the police force, then the inputs used are labor and capital. The capital consists of squad cars, computers, surveillance equipment, and the like. If a law enforcement agency were operated as a profit-seeking business, it would utilize a mix of labor and machines such that the last dollar spent on each would yield the same marginal product. One of the difficulties in analyzing the mix of crime prevention resources as they apply to different types of crimes is that the value of the output is often unknown. That is to say, no one can objectively say that the prevention of a robbery is more desirable than the prevention of an illicit drug transaction.

DISCUSSION QUESTIONS

1. Discuss the allocation of resources of other non-market activities, such as higher education, fire-fighting, or highway construction.
2. How does a firm decide how to allocate resources? How does it differ from a government agency?

19

the economics of
More Taxes and Less Work

Back in the early days of the Reagan administration, one attempt to avoid the twin evils of **inflation** and unemployment was **supply-side economics**, popularly called "Reaganomics." The emphasis of supply-side economics is on the relationship between taxes and income. Essentially, supply-siders maintain that the higher the marginal tax rate, the lower the amount of work (and, consequently, income) that is forthcoming. Therefore, if the government would just tax us less, we would work more. Ultimately, the government would benefit in the form of higher tax revenues because incomes would be so much higher. But does this, in fact, really happen? On its surface, the essence of supply-side economics cannot be faulted. After all, most supply curves slope upward. That is to say, at higher prices, a larger quantity is forthcoming. Therefore, if workers are offered higher *net* wages per marginal unit of work effort, won't they work more? The answer is yes, *most of the time*.

In order to understand the qualification, we have to look at the labor-leisure choices that we all make and the economywide supply of labor. Leisure is a good—it generates positive utility for most people. A labor-leisure budget constraint exists for everyone. Think of it in terms of the maximum number of hours (24) available in any one day for "consumption." For every hour worked, an hour of leisure (defined as time spent not working) must be given up. The opportunity cost of leisure time, therefore, is a decrease in money income. Put another way, the opportunity cost for leisure is the sacrificed goods and services that extra money income could buy. If a net wage rate is $10 per hour, an extra hour of leisure would cost $10—or $10 worth of goods and services.

A *proportional* tax on all labor income reduces the opportunity cost of leisure by an equal amount. For example, if a worker is now earning $10 an hour, a 25-percent income tax on all labor income earned would lower the after-tax wage rate to $7.50 an hour, regardless of the number of hours worked. A *progressive* income tax takes a bigger and bigger bite out of labor income earned, so the opportunity cost of leisure becomes lower as a worker works more and therefore moves into increasingly high tax brackets. Thus, both a proportional and a progressive income tax lower the after-tax income and therefore lower the opportunity cost of leisure, but by differing amounts at different numbers of hours worked.

It seems straightforward that an increase in tax rates would decrease the number of hours worked. And if this is so, the converse should also be true—that is, a reduction in tax rates should increase the number of hours worked and, consequently, total income in the economy. This would be the logical result of what we have been examining: the **substitution effect** of a change in the price of working. As tax rates fall, workers substitute work for leisure.

But there is another effect that is occurring at the same time. It can be best illustrated by what happened to American companies that embarked upon large-scale development projects in Algeria when that country became independent from France in 1962. Wage rates in Algeria at the time were perhaps one-tenth of what they were in the United States for comparable work. Although American companies weren't about to pay Algerian laborers American wages, they saw no reason to pay what seemed to be the abysmally low wages commonly received by manual laborers in that country. Instead, they offered a wage rate that was perhaps one-third of what it would be in the United States but effectively three to four times more than what the normal Algerian wage earner typically made. Now, supply-side economics would lead us to predict that at those comparably high wage rates, Algerian laborers would want to work more, not less. But this didn't happen. Much to the chagrin of the American managers, large parts of their labor force would simply not show up for work after having worked a short period of time. Why not? Because those workers had obtained the equivalent of one or two years' worth of income in a very short period. Therefore, they could afford to "buy" large amounts of leisure—which they chose to do.

What the American companies experienced was what economists call the **income effect** of a change in wages. At some point, the individual's supply curve of labor is backward bending. That is, after effective after-tax wage rates are increased to higher and higher levels, an income effect takes place: The increased income makes a person feel richer and thus that individual is motivated to buy more leisure, not less—even though the opportunity cost of buying more leisure has increased. When this income effect overrides the substitution effect, the individual's labor supply curve becomes backward bending. Thus, we would predict that if marginal tax rates are decreased more and more, they will eventually cause workers to work less, not more.

The Reagan administration used supply-side theory in

making the policy conclusion that tax rates should be cut, particularly for higher-income groups, to produce more economic activity and thereby more tax revenue. The enactment in 1981 of the Kemp-Roth tax plan, which reduced income taxes by 25 percent in three stages, was the legislative highlight of supply-side economics. But the very large deficits that resulted when the economy did not rebound quickly from the recession of the early 1980s called into question the practical effects of supply-side theory, and the Reagan administration retreated from sole reliance on tax reductions to stimulate economic growth. Nonetheless, the administration still hoped that other tax-reform measures in the 1980s, particularly the Tax Reform Act of 1986, would result not only in a fairer taxation system, but also, in the long run, in increased revenues for government as a result of slightly lower overall tax rates for the majority of taxpayers. Unfortunately, as yet we don't have much evidence on which to base predictions on how effective supply-side economics might be if, in fact, marginal tax rates were significantly lowered for most of the American population.

SUMMARY

The essence of supply-side economics is that the higher the marginal tax rate, the lower the amount of work (and income) that is forthcoming. This is because laborers will substitute more leisure for labor when the opportunity cost of leisure is lowered—as it is when wages are effectively lowered by higher marginal tax rates. Conversely, at higher after-tax wage rates, individuals will work more, as the opportunity cost of leisure is also higher. At a certain point, however, this substitution effect is overridden by the income effect. That is, at higher levels of income, individuals are more motivated to purchase more leisure time—even when the opportunity cost of leisure is also higher. A good illustration of the income effect was the response of Algerian workers to the relatively high wage rates offered by American firms in that country in the 1960s: After a short period of time, the Algerian workers opted for more leisure in spite of the high wage rate and, thus, the high opportunity cost of leisure.

DISCUSSION QUESTIONS

1. What other substitution effects can result from high marginal tax rates? (Hint: What about do-it-yourself projects around the home?)
2. Do you think that the Tax Reform Act of 1986 will create increased tax revenues in the long run because of the lower overall tax rates for the majority of American taxpayers?

part four
Social Issues and Externalities

INTRODUCTION

Many issues in our society do not seem to lend themselves to strict supply-demand analysis. Typically these issues involve what are called *externalities*, that is, either the costs or the benefits—or both—of some economic activity are external to the decision-making process of those who are generating them. An example of a negative externality is air pollution. Externalities, whether they be negative or positive, typically occur because of a common property problem. **Common property** is property that at one and the same time is owned by no one and by everyone. Air and, to a lesser extent, water have been treated as common property for many years. Since no one effectively owns common property, no one has an incentive to efficiently use (or not abuse) it.

The lack of property rights is the central issue in the chapters on animal extinction, oil spills, and clamming. And the externality of urban transportation problems is related to taxicab-licensing restrictions in Chapter 23. These are all social issues involving **social costs** and benefits. An explicit attempt to create property rights in the ability to pollute is discussed in Chapter 24, while Chapter 25 offers a cost/benefit analysis of crime and punishment.

All of the issues discussed in this part demonstrate the power of economic analysis. Social issues have a way of becoming economic issues, because they typically involve decisions about how to use scarce resources.

20

the economics of
Animal Extinction

In its report on the Endangered Species Act of 1973, the Senate Commerce Committee concluded that the two major causes of animal extinction are hunting and destruction of habitat. There is certainly an element of truth in this observation: Ever since prehistoric times humans and animals have competed for space and habitat on this planet. The problem, however, is more complex than a simple statement of that sort.

   Let us begin with prehistoric times. The destruction of animal species by humans is nothing new. The arrival of human beings in North America about 12,000 years ago is usually tied to the extinction of most of the existing megafauna. The LaBrea Tarpits yielded 24 mammals and 22 birds that no longer exist. Among these are the saber-tooth tiger, the giant llama, the 20-foot ground sloth, a bison that stands 7 feet at the hump with 6-foot wide horns, and so on.

In fact, only 0.02 percent of all of the species that have ever existed on earth are currently extant. While many believe that human hunting was directly responsible for the destruction of these species, there is some evidence to the contrary.

The argument for direct human guilt in destroying these animals is based on the view that humans were indiscriminate, wasteful hunters. Hunting methods such as driving animals over a cliff, which resulted in many more being killed than could be used by the tribe, are illustrations of this indiscriminate destruction of male and female animals alike. The fact that no group had exclusive property rights over animals meant that there was no incentive to husband the resource. If one group was careful and husbanded the animals, another group would simply exploit them in competition with that group.

This view has not gone unchallenged. Some have argued that, in fact, primitive tribes did husband the resource and attempted to kill off only the weaker animals, saving the females of the species. But note that the issue was still one over property rights. To the degree that the animals were exclusively within the hunting range of only one tribe, that tribe had an incentive to husband the resource and to provide for a perpetual renewal of those animals.

Whether or not primitive tribes in America were responsible for the extinction of many early animals and birds is still an open question, but the role of human beings in the extinction of animals at a later time is much clearer. The first known instance is the extinction of the European lion, the last survivor being dated to A.D. 80. In modern times the most famous example is that of the passenger pigeon. At one time these birds were the most numerous species of birds in North America and perhaps in the world. They nested and migrated together in huge flocks, and may have numbered more than a billion. When flocks passed overhead the sky would be dark with pigeons, literally for days at a time. Audubon measured one roost at 40 miles long and about 3 miles wide. While the Indians had long hunted these birds, it was the arrival of the white man and the demand for pigeons as a food source that led to their ultimate demise. The birds were netted in vast numbers. And by the end of the nineteenth century, an animal species that had been looked upon as literally indestructible because of its enormous numbers had almost completely disappeared. The last known passenger pigeon died in the Cincinnati zoo in 1914.

The American bison only narrowly escaped the same fate. The vast herds that roamed the plains were an easy target for hunters; with the advent of the railroad and the need to feed railroad crews as transcontinental railroad lines were built, hunters such as Buffalo Bill Cody killed bison by the thousands. Then, as the demand for the fur of the bison increased, it became the target for still further hunting. Like the passenger pigeon, the bison appeared to be indestructible because of its numbers. But in the absence of any property rights over bison, the result was almost the same as with the passenger pigeon—bison were becoming extinct. Despite the outcries of the Indians who found their major food source being decimated, it was not until late in the nineteenth century that any efforts were made to protect the bison.

The fate of the passenger pigeon and of the bison illustrates the main dilemma of protecting endangered species. To the degree that there are no ownership rights over these animals, anyone can attempt to hunt them for private gain. The conflict between the needs of human beings for food or clothing and the survival of a particular species can only lead to one end—the extinction of the animal species.

In modern times, government has attempted, by means of state and federal regulation, to limit hunting seasons and the number of animals or birds that may be taken. The results have been at least partially successful. It is probable that there are more deer in North America today than there were at the time of the colonists. The same is true for a number of other animal species. In effect, a rationing system (rather than prices) was used to limit the exploitation of a "common property resource." But the threatened extinction in modern times of many species of whales illustrates that the problem is far from resolved.

The pattern of harvesting whales has been the subject of international discussion ever since World War II; it was readily apparent to all concerned that without some form of restraint the whaling population was in danger of extinction. The result was the setting up of an international regulatory body, the International Whaling Commission (IWC), in 1948, in an attempt to regulate international whaling through co-operative endeavor. But the IWC was virtually doomed from the start. Its members were given the right to veto any regulation they considered too restrictive; if a member decided to blatantly disobey regulations, the IWC had no enforcement powers. Since some whaling nations, such as Chile and Peru, refused to join the IWC, quotas had little effect on these nations. And some IWC members have used non-member flagships to circumvent the quotas themselves.

The story of the decimation of a species is probably best told in the events surrounding the blue whale. Even with the most modern equipment, the great blue whale, which sometimes weighs almost a hundred tons, is difficult to kill; nevertheless intensive hunting methods gradually reduced the stock from somewhere between 300,000 and 1,000,000 to, at present, somewhere between 600 and 3000. In the 1930–1931 winter season almost 30,000 blue whales were taken. By 1945–1946, fewer than 10,000 were taken, and in the late 1950s the yearly catch was down to around 1500 per year. By 1964–1965, the total was only 20 whales. In 1965, a ban was placed by the IWC on killing blue whales. But even after the ban, the hunting of blues continued from land stations by nonmembers such as Brazil, Chile, and Peru.

Humpback whales have suffered a similar fate. From an original population estimated at 300,000, there remain between 1500 and 5000 today. Like the blues, humpbacks are now under a hunting ban, but the lack of monitoring capacity makes it probable that the ban is only nominal. The problems of the IWC can be seen in the reactions to several conservation measures passed at the 1973 meeting. The United States pushed through measures banning the hunting of finbacks in the Antarctic, setting the quota on minke whales at 5000 instead of 12,000 as Japan requested, and instituting an area by area quota for sperm whales so that the total population would be protected. A year later, the Japanese and then the Russians, parties to these agreements, announced they would set more realistic quotas in line with Japanese interests.

Moreover, even where government regulations attempt to protect animals, poaching, a lucrative source of income, has been widespread. This is particularly true in poor nations: To an individual native hunter in Africa, the income from the ivory tusks of a single elephant may be the difference between starvation and relative abundance.

Nothing better illustrates the dilemma of animal extinction than the cases of the snail darter and of the coyote. The National Environmental Policy Act of 1969 made it mandatory that an environmental impact statement be made on all projects that would affect the environment. A mechanism was thus created for the protection of endangered species against environmental destruction. The most famous example involves the snail darter, a small fish whose existence was threatened by the construction of a dam proposed by the Tennessee Valley Authority (TVA). The environmental impact statement process required the TVA to list the extinction of the snail darter as the probable outcome of the construction of the dam. The 1973 Endangered Species Act, with its clause requiring emergency action to protect any species threatened with extinction, was invoked. The result was a national furor in which the benefits to humankind of the additional power to be provided by the dam were measured against the possible extinction of an obscure small fish, the existence of which was known only to a very small number of people. In fact, this issue was resolved when the TVA reevaluated the benefit costs of the dam and concluded that it was not worthwhile after all. Nevertheless, many people viewed the conflict as an absurd one in terms of the benefit costs of a snail darter versus hydroelectric power.

However, if the snail darter illustrates an absurdity in the efforts to save animals from extinction, the case of coyote versus sheep highlights a more difficult dilemma. The coyote has not come under protection, but the ways by which it can be hunted have been severely limited; in particular, some methods of poisoning the coyote have been restricted or forbidden, with the result that there has been an enormous growth in their population.

Lamb is a favorite food of the coyote. Consequently, the sheepherders in many areas have found it prohibitively expensive to raise sheep because of their ravaging by a growing coyote population. With fewer sheep, the relative prices of wool and lamb have risen significantly in the United States. What should be the outcome? Should the coyote be protected, as many environmental groups have insisted, and are we willing to pay the price of substantially higher costs for wool and lamb as a result? The conflict between human and animal species is not easily resolved, as these two cases illustrate.

SUMMARY

If one were to draw up two separate lists of animals—those that are endangered and those that are not—one would be hard pressed to come up with a single set of physical characteristics distinguishing the two. In actuality, the main distinction between endangered animals and nonendangered ones is that the former are common property. There is no incentive for a single individual to refrain from killing common property animals, because the action will have no effect on the total number of animals that ultimately survive. All of the government restrictions on hunting are an attempt to overcome the common property problem. Unfortunately, even government restrictions are hard to enforce in the case of animals that are constantly on the move, such as the whale.

DISCUSSION QUESTIONS

1. Has there ever been a problem of the extinction of dogs, cats, or cattle? Why not?
2. Some argue that the only way to save rare species is to set up private game reserves to which wealthy hunters can travel. How could this help save endangered species?

21

the economics of
Oil Pollution

On the night of March 16, 1978, the supertanker *Amoco Cadiz* encountered stormy seas off the Brittany coast of France. Losing control of its rudder, the tanker ran aground and split apart. The result was the costliest maritime accident ever: The $15-million ship was lost and 68 million gallons of crude oil spilled into the icy sea. An oil slick 18 miles wide and 80 miles long polluted 130 miles of the French coastline. In April of 1984, six years later, Chicago federal district judge Frank J. McGarr ruled that Standard Oil Company (Amoco) and the two subsidiaries operating the tanker were liable for most of the damages caused by the spill. These damages are estimated at nearly $2 billion.

Until a few years ago, the term *oil pollution* inevitably called to mind a scene such as the above and seas and coastal areas polluted by oil slicks. In the mid-1970s, when escalating oil prices created a demand for cheaper ways of transporting crude oil, supertankers began to emerge as the solution. Some of these sea mammoths cost as much as $100 million to build and were so large that crew members used motorbikes to get from one end of the ship to the other. The largest was nearly one-third of a mile long and weighed nearly 565 thousand tons. Accidental oil spills from these enormous tankers—such as the one in 1978 and several earlier ones—caused scientists and others to become gravely concerned about the welfare of our planet's oceans and marine life.

In recent years, however, the threat of oil spills from supertankers has been reduced by forces in the marketplace. As a result of the steady decline in oil prices over the past several years, these supertankers are rapidly becoming obsolete. Increasingly, they are being replaced by more profitable smaller tankers and are leaving the high seas to be disassembled in wrecking yards or used for storage. According to a recent report by the National Research Council, oil spills now are believed to contribute less to the petroleum content in our oceans than do routine tanker operations and municipal and other wastes.

Of greater concern today is the pollution of our groundwater supplies by gasoline and other petroleum products caused by leakage from underground storage tanks. Studies show that the "safe" life of an underground steel tank is approximately 15 years and that at least half of all the tanks that have been underground for a longer period are now leaking. One oil industry expert has estimated that nearly one-third of the nation's approximately 1.2 million service-station tanks may be leaking today.

This **negative externality** of the retail oil industry is a costly one for water users. Health hazards caused by drinking gasoline-polluted water include anemia, kidney disease, disorders of the nervous system, and cancer. Even bathing in such polluted water can be harmful. For example, benzene—one of the nearly 300 chemicals contained in gasoline—can be absorbed through the skin during a bath. The result of such a bath would be the same as it would be if you drank benzene-polluted water. Showering in such water also can cause chemical vapors that may result in skin and eye irritation.

The problem of this form of water pollution is complicated by the fact that underground water is essentially a *common-property resource*. To a certain extent, it is like air: Nobody owns it and everybody can use it. This means that a service-station owner, for example, even if that proprietor knew that an underground gas tank was old and very likely leaking, would have no incentive to incur the high cost of replacing the tank unless he or she were being affected by the polluted water. We would hope that the gas-station owner would let humane motives govern his or her actions and replace the tank to prevent further water pollution, even though it would prove very costly. Unfortunately, economic theory predicts that unless the benefits to an individual from a potential action outweigh the costs, that action will very likely not be undertaken. And unless health of the service-station owner in this case is immediately threatened by the water being polluted, the benefits may not be perceived to be greater than the costs.

What can be done to keep further oil pollution from occurring? One obvious solution is to make the polluters pay in the form of liability lawsuits for damages. But determining who the polluting culprit is can sometimes be a difficult matter, especially in a large metropolitan area where several underground tanks are located in the same vicinity. Assessing the costs in this case is also complicated. How do you place a price tag on illnesses caused by water pollution? And how can it be demonstrated, beyond a reasonable doubt, that certain illnesses are the result of polluted water and not some other factor? In principle, these determinations can be made. But in practice, the task is far from simple.

An even more obvious solution is to enact state or federal legislation mandating the replacement of all underground tanks every 15 years. Such legislation, however, would not be without costs to society. One of the consequences of such laws would be the increased taxes necessary to pay for the policing and enforcement of replacement requirements. Another cost would be a higher price for gasoline. This is because the purchase and installation of new gas tanks is a very costly undertaking, and those additional costs incurred by oil companies and service-station owners would be passed on to the consumer. Rich and poor alike use gasoline, but it represents a larger proportion of the expenditures of the poor.[1] Hence, a greater burden would fall on low-income groups. Legislation of this type would also very likely mean the disappearance of many of the smaller service-stations that are owned and operated by independent dealers who can ill afford the additional cost required by tank replacements. The million or so independent dealers currently in business across the nation offer competition to the major oil companies and a convenience to Americans that may have to be reduced if such laws were passed.

In short, a solution to the problem or oil pollution of our underground water supply is not simple, nor is it likely to be without cost. Whether we like it or not, safe drinking water is becoming a scarce good, and like other scarce commodities, it may well have a higher price tag in the future.

SUMMARY

Until recently, oil spills resulting from supertanker accidents were perceived as one of the major threats to our planet's water sources. Because steadily declining oil prices have decreased the number of supertankers, however, oil spills are no longer the major problem they were in the past. Concern

[1]Studies have shown the following distribution of gasoline expenditures as a proportion of annual income: $6000–$10,000 income, 3.4 percent; $10,000–$14,000 income, 3.3 percent; $14,000–$30,000 income, less than 2 percent; above $30,000, 1.4 percent.

is now focused on the pollution of our groundwater supplies caused by leaking tanks containing gasoline and other petroleum products. One solution to the problem is to make polluters pay, in the form of liability lawsuits, for damages they cause to innocent users of polluted water. This would prove difficult, although not necessarily impossible, because it is sometimes hard to identify the polluter and damages caused to water users are hard to assess. Another solution is to pass legislation mandating replacement requirements for aged tanks; but this solution would not be without cost to Americans, as it is likely to result in higher taxes and higher gasoline prices. Effectively, safe water, like other scarce goods, would carry a higher price tag.

DISCUSSION QUESTIONS

1. Can you think of solutions, other than government legislation, to the problem of underground water pollution?
2. Does the problem of water pollution differ in any way from the problem of air pollution?

22

the economics of
Clamming and Other "Free" Goods

The razor clam (*Siliqua patula*) is a large bivalve of the So-
lenidae family that inhabits the ocean beaches of the Pacific
Coast from California to Alaska. Once a major staple of the
coastal Indian population, it is now a major prey of the people escaping the city for the ocean beaches. (Cleaned, cut
into steaks, dipped in batter, fried one minute on each side,
and served with a bottle of dry white wine, it is superb.)

These clams are dug in minus tides, and the beach area
they inhabit is not, at least in the state of Washington, private property. Therefore, access is available to everyone, and
the only costs of digging clams are cut fingers and an oc-
casional dunking in icy water. Nobody owns them; they are
a common-property resource, a **free good.** But this fact does
not make clams any less subject to economic analysis than
goods with price tags on them. A **demand schedule** exists

for clamming. Like other demand schedules, it shows that more people will use more of the product at a low price than at a high one; and that how *much* more they use will depend on **elasticity of demand** (that is, degree of responsiveness to a given change in price). When the price is zero, as it was in clamming until the summer of 1979, the amount used will certainly be much more than at any level of positive price. Again, how much more depends on the elasticity of the demand schedule.

We can also derive, hypothetically at least, a supply curve, although to discover positive prices we would have to envision private ownership of beaches and see how many clams would be offered by beach owners at various prices. The higher the price, the more would be offered. Presumably, if the price were right, the owner would incur costs of "cultivating" and protecting clam beds to increase their yield.

If a market situation existed, an equilibrium price and quantity could be established; but since a wide gap is inevitable between the amount demanded at zero price and the amount supplied at zero price, some device must ration the product. State authorities take on this task by setting daily catch limits and closing certain seasons to clamming. Regulations for the state of Washington first allowed non-commercial diggers to take 15 clams a day on any ocean beach from midnight to noon between March 16 and June 30. Unfortunately, these regulations were only a short-run solution. In the distant past, when the Pacific Coast was sparsely settled, no particular problem existed (in fact, no limit or season was set, since in those days, even at a zero price, the supply exceeded the demand).[1] But each year more and more people have more income for traveling to beaches

---

[1]By 1925, regulations did limit commercial harvesting of Washington razor clams to the months of March, April, and May. A well-trained clam digger can remove as much as half a ton of clams during one low tide. There was no need then to restrict the season for noncommercial clam digging.

and more leisure to devote to clamming. The result is that the demand keeps increasing, and each year happy clam hunters crowd the minus-tide beaches. In Oregon, the clam-seeking camper sometimes faces lines as much as a mile long.

The supply also may increase if new beaches are opened up or if the State Fisheries Department attempts to cultivate more clams on existing beaches. But the increase can be only minimal once all the beaches have been made accessible. The ultimate result must inevitably be more crowding and fewer clams each year. It is not a happy prospect.

The clamming story is repeated over and over again for recreational activities, and the same analysis applies. In the case of wilderness areas, the supply is actually decreasing rather than merely remaining constant. All over the country, fishing, hunting, and camping sites are overcrowded, although these areas have somewhat greater potential for expansion of supply.

What is being done to improve the situation? A price is charged for fishing and hunting in the form of license fees, and more recently camping sites in parks are being "rented." In 1979, the Washington state legislature finally established a $2.50 resident (and $10 nonresident) clamming license. In each case, however, the rates have been set so far below the equilibrium price, which could balance quantities supplied with quantities demanded, that they are not even close to resolving the problem of overcrowding. And each year it gets worse. Anyone wishing to test the proposition need only visit Yellowstone or Yosemite National Park in the summer.

Contrast the case of clams with that of the oyster beds in the state of Washington, which were privately owned before the state restricted private ownership of tidal land. Those oyster beds were treated as an asset in which investment was made to improve the yield. In fact, the oysters are farmed just like any other agricultural commodity. Perhaps a more spectacular contrast is between the north and south shores of Chesapeake Bay. On the north shore, the state of Maryland has made the oyster beds a common-property resource; as would be expected where entry is unlimited, severe depletion has occurred. Moreover, it has not been worthwhile to invest privately in improving the yield. In order to cut down on the harvest, the state has forced the use of archaic harvesting tools and archaic propulsion requirements (that is, oyster dredging can only be done under sail power). In contrast, the state of Virginia on the south shore of the bay allows private ownership of tidal lands. With 80 percent of the tidal land in private hands, owners have developed the oyster beds into a thriving sustained enterprise. The average output per worker was 59 percent higher in Virginia than in Maryland during the 25-year period 1945–1969.[2]

Why are we content with a zero, or now a nominal, price for clamming or for fishing? The answer is that the American people have long believed that such activities are a hereditary right, that they should be equally accessible to rich and poor alike, and that charging a fee favors the rich (which it certainly does). This argument prevails in the cases of clamming, fishing, and hunting, but not in the case of buying yachts and airplanes. The result is to artificially lower the price for a particular publicly owned commodity—clams—but not for all commodities. In effect, the public policy is saying that income should not be a factor in people's ability to clam or to fish, but that it can be in buying golf clubs, TV sets, or airplanes. In effect, this is a policy of selective income redistribution.

As crowding, rationing, and queuing become more and more severe in such nonpriced or underpriced activities, it becomes a major issue to determine whether rationing by

[2]Richard J. Agnello and Lawrence P. Donnelley, "Property Rights and Efficiency in the Oyster Industry," *Journal of Law and Economics*, vol.18, no. 2 (October 1975), p. 531.

price or by quantity restriction is the better method. One alternative is to eliminate the common-property aspects of such resources. Another is for the government to set a price that approximates a market price. The final alternaive consists of a variety of rationing devices to restrict quantity more and more rigidly.

SUMMARY

Some have called common-property resources "free" goods. Actually, the fact that a resource is common property does not mean it is free. It may only be free in the sense that the explicit monetary price that is paid is zero. The cost to society is, of course, always going to be greater than zero, provided that the quantity supplied at a zero price is less than the quantity demanded. Because an excess quantity is demanded at a zero price, the state imposes regulations to prevent the overconsumption of "free" goods such as clams. Also, user fees have been imposed, but they are typically well below a price that would equate quantity demanded with quantity supplied.

DISCUSSION QUESTIONS

1. Clams are not really "free" goods, but rather goods sold at a low or zero price. Are there, in fact, any truly free goods in our society?
2. In the case of oysters, there seems to be no problem of overconsumption. What is the difference between the farming of clams and oysters?

23

the economics of
Taxis and Jitneys

The fact that you probably never heard the word "jitney" says something about the problems we wish to pose in this chapter. Jitneys, to all intents and purposes, disappeared from the urban American scene some time ago. But jitneys and taxis have formed a major basis of the transportation in urban areas at various times. For our purposes they illustrate a major dilemma on the transportation scene: the use of political policies and regulatory devices in municipalities to restrict or eliminate certain kinds of competition, with consequences for the overall efficiency of transportation in America.

The dictionary defines a jitney as a "bus or car, especially one traveling a regular route, that carries passengers for a small fare, originally five cents." Believe it or not, there are a few places in the United States where jitneys still exist, and they are still a common form of transportation in many foreign cities, such as in Mexico City, along the Paseo de la Reforma, where they are called *peseros*. The principle of a jitney is simple. A vehicle, usually a normal-sized sedan but sometimes a small minibus, travels along a usually fixed route, picking up customers anywhere along that route until the vehicle is filled and dropping those customers off wherever they designate along that fixed route. In a modified situation, the jitney will (for an additional fee, of course) take a customer off the route but within a limited range, only to return to the point of deviation for continuance along the same route. The difference between a jitney and a regular taxi is that the latter cannot generally pick up more than one paying set of customers at a time and does not follow a fixed route. (As we shall see, these restrictions are usually imposed by law, not by the taxi drivers.)

Jitneys appeared on the American transportation scene prior to our entry into World War I. When they first appeared, they offered advantages over the then-prevalent mode of public transportation—electric street railways—the chief one being a higher average speed. That speed of 15 miles an hour was still twice as fast as streetcar speeds. Jitneys were also allowed greater flexibility in their routes as compared with the absolutely fixed route of street railways.

The advantages of jitneys were sufficient at the prices charged for them to pose a serious competitive threat to electric railway systems throughout the United States. In fact the *Electric Railway Journal* started calling jitneys "a menace," the "Frankenstein of transportation," and various other epithets. A competing mode of transportation threatened to erode the profits of railway systems in municipalities. A general rule of thumb is: If when faced with competition you cannot compete on an economic basis, try the political arena. That is exactly what the railways did—they sought protection from the governments of the municipalities in which they were located. In spite of scattered newspaper support for pro-jitney political policies, the efforts of jitney association lobbyists, and the obviously anticompetitive implications of antijitney legislation, restrictive legislation was passed throughout the United States.

At first the legislation required jitney operators to obtain licenses to use public streets as a place of business. This restriction drastically reduced the ease of entering the business, particularly since the municipalities made it a lengthy and costly procedure to obtain the permit or license. In some cities a license or franchise had to be submitted to voters! Additional costs were imposed, such as the requirement that relatively large liability bonds be purchased to protect the consumer of jitney services should a wrong be committed against him by a jitney operator. In some cases, the cost of licensing fees plus bonding requirements equaled 50 percent of a jitney driver's annual earnings. This is the equivalent of a tax in that amount on drivers. In a highly competitive industry, in which the individual participants were not making excessive profits, such a tax could only lead to one result—the elimination of a significant fraction of the industry's participants.

Further restrictions were added that basically eliminated the jitney as a form of public transportation in the United States. These included a requirement that any jitney had to be operated a minimum number of hours, that minimum usually exceeding the average number of hours that jitneys were usually run; the fixing of routes and schedules, which eliminated the flexibility that jitneys offered; and the exclusion of jitneys from high-density downtown areas and specifically from trolley routes—the most advantageous working locations for the jitney drivers.[1] According to L. R.

---

[1] In 1974 the Los Angeles City Council removed its prohibition on jitney service. However, a proposed ordinance was soon put forth allowing the municipal bus system to restrict jitneys from operating along major bus routes. The city bus system successfully quashed plans to allow jitneys along heavily traveled routes. (History repeats itself.)

Nash,[2] a student of jitney history, within 18 months of the appearance of jitneys in Los Angeles, antijitney (i.e., pro-trolley) regulatory ordinances had been passed in 125 of the 175 cities in which jitneys competed with trolleys. Most major municipalities acted similarly within another year.

The elimination of the jitney industry certainly benefited the electric trolleys, but it also benefited the taxi industry, which we present as another example of restricted competition.

In most cities in the United States, not just anyone can legally drive a taxi, and those who drive one legally are restricted in many ways. Most importantly, they are restricted to specific geographic areas and in the price they charge a customer. That price is generally regulated by a commission and is uniform at all times of day for all taxis.

In the taxi business in many cities, the potential owner-operator of a cab must purchase what is called a medallion. The ownership of this medallion gives the owner the legal right to operate a taxi within a specified area. So far so good. However, for example, in New York City the price of these medallions has at times gone up to $65,000 and the price has reached similarly astronomical heights in other cities. How, you might ask, could the right to operate a taxicab cost so much? Clearly, the medallion is inexpensive to produce, even if it is made out of bronze.

The key to understanding this issue is understanding that there is generally a *fixed* number of medallions available. In other words, entry into the taxicab business in many cities in the United States is limited by law to zero. That is the only reason a medallion owner can sell his or her rights to the taxicab operation to another person for such a high figure. The person buying the medallion would not pay such a price unless he or she was fairly certain that no new com-

---

[2]L.R. Nash, "History and Economics of the Jitney," *Stone and Webster Journal*, vol. 18 (1916), pp. 361, 365.

petition would exist in the future and that present monopoly rates of return, or profits, would continue into the indefinite future for any owner of a medallion. Naturally, those monopoly profits can only exist so long as the monopoly exists, and in a situation in which potential entry merely involves putting a sign on a four-door sedan reading "Taxi for Hire," the possibility of competition—eliminating any monopoly profits—is great. Only legislation designed for preventing entry can effectively ward off competition; that is, the police power of the state must be used to protect the monopoly position of individuals in the taxicab business. The documentation on the legislation perpetuating monopolies in cities such as Los Angeles, Dallas, Fort Worth, Philadelphia, Cleveland, New York, and Chicago is impressive, undeniably illustrating a classic case of restricted entry.

As you might expect, if the number of taxicabs is too severely limited, the potential for cheaters or interlopers in the existing monopoly situation is great. In fact, the "problem" of illegal or "gypsy" cabs operating in New York City is well known. Apparently officials turn a more or less deaf ear to this problem, recognizing that the limitation on the number of medallions has become too severe given the growing population of the city. The same is true in Chicago, where the gypsies are occasionally picked up but only fined $100. In general, there seems to be more toleration of illegal taxicabs in ghetto areas in New York, St. Louis, Pittsburgh, and perhaps Chicago. In such areas, there is a demand for taxis because of the diffuse home-work situations. Moreover, there is a relatively large supply of illegal taxicabs and taxicab operators because of the large number of unemployed individuals living in those sections who know how to drive.

It has been suggested that a way to solve urban transportation problems would be to lift the restrictions against jitneys and against the proliferation of taxis by removing legislation prohibiting individuals from going into business for themselves. Note, however, that if this were done, all current owners of taxi licenses would suffer windfall losses. After all, those who benefited from restriction on entry into the business were the *original* owners of the licenses or the monopoly rights. The current owners had to pay a competitive price to obtain those rights, and that price included all future monopoly profits that the original owners perceived would exist. Current owners only make a normal rate of return, and they would suffer losses if the valuable asset—the medallion—that they purchased at a price of, say $25,000, became worth zero.

Another possibility is to lift all restrictions on taxicab and jitney operations in certain cities while compensating current owners of monopoly rights for their windfall losses. If this were to occur, the urban transportation mess might be ameliorated, though it certainly would not be solved.

SUMMARY

Jitneys were put out of business in the United States through the political activities of municipal railway systems. Today, an additional political force preventing their reemergence in most cities is the taxicab monopoly. In many major cities, taxi ownership interests have succeeded in establishing a monopoly market structure in which only those who have a medallion (license) can legally operate a taxicab or a fleet of taxicabs. The value of the medallion on the open market is equivalent to the (discounted) profits over and above the competitive rate of return. In New York City, it has at times had a value as high as $65,000. Open competition in the taxicab market, or effective competition by illegal gypsy cabs, would reduce the value of the medallion severely. In the extreme case, it would have a zero value.

DISCUSSION QUESTIONS

1. What are some of the justifications for taxicab licensing?
2. What would happen to the market value of medallions if jitneys were allowed?

24

the economics of
Selling
Pollution Rights

Pollution, almost by definition, is undesirable. The Environmental Protection Agency (EPA) measures pollution in terms of ozone content because of the harmful effects of ozone on human health. Ozone, a large component of smog, results when vapors from oil products and solvents mix with nitrogen oxides and other gases on warm, sunny days. The effect of ozone on humans can range from less effective lung function to coughing, asthma attacks, and chest pain in deep breathing.

   In 1986, EPA standards barred ozone concentrations from exceeding 0.12 parts per million more than once a year. Some scientists feel, however, that even below this concentration, ill effects can occur. And some animal studies suggest that long-term exposure to even lower levels of ozone concentration may result in lasting damage.

There are numerous ways to reduce or avoid pollution. Laws can be passed banning production processes that emit pollutants into the air and water or specifying a minimum air quality level or the maximum amount of pollution allowable. Firms would then be responsible for developing the technology and for paying the price to satisfy such standards. Or the law could specify the particular type of production technology to be used and the type of pollution-abatement equipment required in order to produce legally. Finally, subsidies could be paid to firms that reduce pollution emission or taxes could be imposed on firms that engage in pollution emission.

No matter which methods are used to reduce pollution, problems will arise. For example, setting physical limits on the amount of pollution permitted would discourage firms from developing the technology that would limit pollution beyond those limits. The alternative of subsidizing firms that reduce pollution levels may seem a strange use of taxpayers' dollars. The latest "solution" to the air pollution problem—selling the rights to pollute—may seem even stranger. Nonetheless, this approach is now being used in the majority of states. Men like Stewart Rupp of Richmond, California, a partner in an environmental consulting firm, work as brokers, helping companies trade the right to pollute.

To understand how this situation came about, we must understand the Federal Clean Air Act. This act was passed in 1963 in an attempt to force a reduction in pollution, particularly in metropolitan areas in the United States. Through rules and regulations of the EPA, the Clean Air Act presents localities with specified permitted pollution levels. These so-called National Air Quality Standards must be met in most major metropolitan areas. However, in many of these areas air quality is already poor. Thus, a company that wishes to build a plant in such an area is theoretically barred from doing so because of its detrimental impact on air quality. If the guidelines were strictly adhered to, it would mean no further industrial growth in many urban areas.

The Environmental Protection Agency approved an off-set policy to get around this problem. A company that wants to build a new plant is required to work out a corresponding reduction in pollution at some existing plant. For example, when Volkswagen wanted to build a plant in New Stanton, Pennsylvania, the state of Pennsylvania agreed to reduce pollutants from its highway-paving operations. This reduction would offset the Volkswagen plant's pollution.

One major problem with the offset policy involves the difficulty in finding an offset partner. In other words, each time a firm wants to build a new plant in an already polluted area, it must seek, on an individual basis, an offset partner that agrees to reduce pollution (usually after a payment from the other company). This is where the idea of brokering the right to pollute comes into play. This is where people like Stewart Rupp can go to work.

A company that closes a plant or installs improved pollution-abatement equipment can receive "emission credits" for its clean-up efforts that can be purchased by another firm. The industry negotiates the price. For example, the Times Mirror Company was able to complete a $120 million expansion of a paper-making plant near Portland, Oregon, after it purchased emission credits allowing it to add 150 tons of extra hydrocarbons into the atmosphere each year. A woodcoating plant and a dry-cleaning firm had gone out of business; they sold the necessary credits for $50,000 to the Times Mirror.

Using a broker to find firms that have emission credits to sell does not solve all the problems with the offset policy. Wisconsin has set up a computer system to track available credits for a nationwide trading system. In Illinois, the chamber of commerce and state environmental office established a clearinghouse to handle a market for the trading of pollution rights. More such centralized marketplaces are sure to spring up, since most states have already adopted regulations or issued permits allowing some form of air pollution offsets.

One of the benefits of a pollution rights "bank," as it

were, is the increased economic incentive to reduce pollution levels below those required by law. A firm that believes it could cheaply reduce pollutants further would find out that at some point another firm would pay it for such a reduction in order to build a new plant. Presumably, such a marketplace for the right to pollute would encourage further research and development in pollution-reduction techniques. Today, many standards are set on an absolute physical basis, offering companies no additional incentive to reduce pollution below the air quality standard.

SUMMARY

A strict physical standard for the amount of air pollution allowable in the atmosphere in any given geographic area can prevent change and growth in a dynamic economy. After all, some firms go out of business and others want to go into business. If each firm has the right to a certain amount of pollution and if it can sell "emission credits," then this problem is surmounted. Under this system, firms that go out of business, firms that develop techniques to reduce pollution, or firms that cut back on production—thereby reducing pollution—can sell their emission credits to firms wanting to expand or to go into business in the same geographical area. Also, if the cost of increased pollution abatement is less than the market price for the emission credits, more pollution abatement will occur per unit of total output produced in the United States.

DISCUSSION QUESTIONS

1. Does marketing the right to pollute mean that we are allowing too much destruction of our environment?
2. Who implicitly has property rights in the air if a pollution bank is set up and the right to pollute is sold to the highest bidder?

25

the economics of
Crime
and
Punishment

Is there a relationship between punishment and the number and types of crimes committed? If so, what are the available alternatives to punishing guilty offenders? Should we impose large fines instead of incarceration? Should we have public whippings? Should capital punishment be allowed? To establish a system of crime deterrence, we would need to assess carefully the value of different supposed deterrents.

One thing we can be sure of. Uniformly heavy punishments for all crimes will lead to a larger number of major crimes being committed. Let's look at the reasoning. All decisions are made on the margin. If an act of theft will be punished by hanging and an act of murder will be punished by the same fate, there is no marginal deterrence to murder. If a theft of $5 is met with a punishment of 10 years in jail and a theft of $50,000 incurs the same sentence, why not steal $50,000? Why not go for broke? There is no marginal deterrence to prevent one from doing so.

A serious question is how our system of justice can establish penalties that are appropriate from a social point of view. To establish the correct (marginal) deterrents, we must observe empirically how criminals respond to changes in punishments. This leads us to the question of how people decide whether to commit a "crime." A theory needs to be established as to what determines the supply of criminal offenses.

Adam Smith once said:

> The affluence of the rich excites the indignation of the poor, who are often both driven by want, and prompted by envy, to invade his possessions. It is only under the shelter of the civil magistrate that the owner of that valuable property, which is acquired by the labour of many years, or perhaps by many successive generations, can sleep a single night in security. He is at all times surrounded by unknown enemies, whom, though he never provokes, he can never appease, and from whose injustice he can be protected only by the powerful arm of the civil magistrate continually held up to chastise it. The acquisition of valuable and extensive property, therefore, necessarily requires the establishment of civil government. Where there is no property, or at least none that exceeds the value of two or three days' labour, civil government is not so necessary.[1]

Smith pointed out that in any society where one person has substantially more property than another, robberies will be committed. We can surmise that the individuals who engage in robberies are seeking income. We can also surmise that, before acting, a professional criminal might be expected to look at the anticipated returns and anticipated costs of criminal activity. These could then be compared with the net returns from legitimate activities. In other words, those en-

---

[1] Adam Smith, *The Wealth of Nations*, 1776.

gaging in crimes do so on the basis of a cost/benefit analysis in which the benefits outweigh the costs. The benefits of the crime of robbery are clear. The cost would include, but not be limited to, apprehension by the police, conviction, and jail. (The criminal's calculations are analogous to those made by a professional athlete when weighing the cost of possible serious injury against the benefits to be gained from participating in the sport.)

If we view the supply of offenses in this manner, we can come up with methods by which society can lower the net expected rate of return for committing any illegal activity. That is, we can figure out how to reduce crime most effectively. We have talked about one particular aspect—the size of penalties. We also briefly mentioned another—the probability of detection for each offense. When either of these costs of crime goes up, the supply of offenses goes down; that is, less crime is committed.

Can this theory be applied to a decision, pro or con, on capital punishment? Sociologists, psychologists, and others have numerous theories correlating the number of murders committed to various psychological, sociological, and demographic variables. In general, they have stressed social and psychological factors as determinants of violent crime and have therefore felt that capital punishment would have no deterrent effect. Economists, on the other hand, have stressed a cost-benefit equation, which implies that capital punishment would deter violent crime.

We start with a commodity called the act of murder. If the act of murder is like any other commodity, the quantity "demanded" (by perpetrators, of course, not victims) will be negatively related to the relative price. But what is the price of murder? Ignoring all the sociological, psychological, or psychic costs of murder, we have to consider the probability of being caught and, after capture, the possible jail sentence or capital punishment that may be called for. But here again, we have to look at the probability of a particular jail sentence and the probability of going to the gas chamber, or the guillotine, or the four winds. Thus, it would do little good to observe the difference in murder rates between states that have capital punishment and states that do not. Instead, we must assess the probability of a convicted murderer actually being executed in those states that do have capital punishment and compare this probability with what happens in states that do not. In some states that allow capital punishment, for example, the probability of a convicted murderer being executed is zero. We find, for example, that a charge of first-degree murder is often changed to a charge of second-degree murder if the penalty for murder is execution. In states that do not allow the death penalty, however, first-degree murder sentences are given more frequently. Recently, it has been argued that "death-qualifying" juries— that is, juries consisting only of persons who do not oppose the death penalty—are more likely to convict individuals of crimes for which the penalty is capital punishment.[2] Because these variables exist among states allowing capital punishment, it is necessary to look at the actual number of executions within a state, and not the laws, in order to establish whether capital punishment is actually a deterrent to murder.

Now, immediately critics of such cost/benefit analysis point to the "fact" that the murderer, either in a moment of unreasoned passion or when confronted with an unanticipated situation (for example, during an armed robbery), does not take into account the expected probability of going to the gas chamber. That is to say, murderers are not acting rationally when they murder. Is this a valid criticism of the economic model of the demand for murder? It is not. If the model predicts poorly, then either the assumptions or the model must be changed. Indeed, if one contends that the expected "price" of committing a murder has no effect on the quantity of murders, one is implicitly negating the law

---

[2]See, for example, the discussion of *Lockhart v. McCree* in "Death Penalty: A Barrier Falls," *Newsweek*, May 19, 1986.

of demand or stating that the price elasticity of the demand for murder is zero. One is also confusing the average murderer with the marginal murderer. All potential murderers do not have to be aware of or react to the change in the expected "price" of committing a murder for the theory to be useful. If a sufficient number of marginal murderers act as if they were responding to the higher expected "price" of murdering, then the demand curve for murders by perpetrators will be downward sloping.

A few economists have actually worked through economic models of the demand for murder and other crimes. One of the first statistical studies of significance is that by Isaac Erlich, published in 1975.[3] One of the variables he included was the objective conditional risk of being executed if caught and convicted of murder. Two elasticities given in one study were −0.06 and −0.065. While these elasticities are relatively small, they are not zero. The implication of these elasticities, given the number of murders and executions in the period covered by the study (1935–1969), was striking. The implied tradeoff between murders and executions was between 7 and 8. "Put differently, an additional execution per year over the period in question may have resulted, on average, in 7 or 8 fewer murders."[4]

The deterrent effect of capital punishment on the crime of murder was more recently also analyzed by Stephen Layson, an economist at the University of North Carolina at Greensboro. His findings are even more suggestive. Layson concluded that every execution of a convicted murderer deters, on average, 18 other murders that would have occurred without it. He also studied the relationship between arrests and convictions of murderers and the murder rate. His conclusions were that a 1-percent increase in the arrest rate for murder would lead to 250 fewer murders per year being

[3]Isaac Erlich,"The Deterrent Effect of Capital Punishment: A Question of Life and Death," *The American Economic Review,* Vol. 65, no. 3 (June 1975). [4]Ibid., p. 414.

committed and that a 1-percent increase in murder convictions would deter about 105 murders.[5]

As might be expected, these findings are highly controversial and have led to a debate that still goes on. Critics have stressed, for example, the tenuous statistical basis of Erlich's findings.[6] While the argument over capital punishment continues, the evidence that crime rates in general appear to vary inversely with estimates of penalties, probabilities of conviction, and legal opportunities has received substantial support.[7] Currently, the arrest rate for murderers is 75 percent; only 38 percent of all murders result in a conviction, and 1 percent of murders result in an execution. It is perhaps not too hard to understand why 75 percent of Americans now favor the death penalty.

One final note. In the case of capital punishment, the execution must be thought to fall on the guilty parties, rather than randomly applied. History tells us that under the emperors in China, executions were frequent. However, the emperors were not always so diligent about executing the right person. This system of "punishment" does little good for society in terms of combating crime, not to mention the loss suffered by the innocent victim and his or her family due to perverted justice.

SUMMARY

One can analyze criminal acts as economic activities. The potential criminal makes an economic decision in which he

[5]Stephen K. Layson, "Homicide and Sentence: A Reexamination of the United States Time-series Evidence," *Southern Economic Journal*, vol. 52 (July 1985), pp. 68–89. For an evaluation of Layson's conclusions, see Ernest Van Den Haag, "Death and Deterrence," *National Review*, (March 14, 1986), p. 16.

[6]Peter Parsell and John R. Taylor, "The Deterrent Effect of Capital Punishment: Another View," *The American Economic Review*, vol. 67, no. 3 (June 1977), pp. 445–451.

[7]Gary Becker and William Landes, editors, *Essays in the Economics of Crime and Punishment* (Columbia University Press: New York, 1974).

or she does a cost/benefit analysis of criminal activities versus legal consequences. A key set of variables in such an analysis involves the costs of criminal activity, which include the costs of getting caught, being sentenced, and suffering punishment. In most major cities, the probabilities of being caught, sentenced, going to trial, and serving time are very low. Hence, when they are multiplied together and the product is multiplied times the potential punishment, the expected cost is extremely small. The potential criminal's cost/benefit analysis therefore often implicitly shows that crime does indeed pay. In order to reduce criminal activities, including murder, an economist would argue that the price paid by the criminal must be increased.

DISCUSSION QUESTIONS

1. The analysis just presented makes the assumption that criminals act rationally. Does the fact that they do not necessarily do so negate our analysis?
2. In many cases, murder is committed among people who know each other. Does this mean that raising the price the murderer has to pay will not affect the quantity of murder demanded by perpetrators?

part five
Political Economy

INTRODUCTION

By now, you are certainly aware that many issues in our society have an economic basis. No matter what the economics of an issue may be, it probably has a political side, too. In fact, the subject matter of political economy is how the body politic decides on the allocation of resources. For the most part, political economy has as its basis different groups of individuals attempting to improve their economic position. Typically, a successful attempt by one group means that another group will suffer a deterioration in its economic position. Otherwise stated, the subject matter of political economy often involves a transfer of wealth among groups in society.

All the issues in this part are political in nature. In Chapter 26 we see how the politics of members of the water board in Santa Barbara, California, effectively created an enormous increase in the market price for existing housing. In the chapters on ecology and government programs, the explicit issue of income distribution is examined, and it is shown that many programs designed to improve the environment and help disadvantaged groups in fact end up improving the economic status of the middle classes and the well-to-do. An economic analysis of black economic progress reveals the political foundation of legislation aimed at helping members of minority groups. Examining the issue of educational vouchers, we learn that those having the most to lose by experimenting with these vouchers are administrators and tenured instructors of relatively low quality who work in the public school systems. They, of course, will use their political clout, principally in the form of lobbying by the National Teachers Association, to prevent a wholesale switch from our current educational system to one utilizing vouchers. Finally, the air pollution caused by smokers is looked at as a classic case of a negative externality, where the cost of smoking also falls on nonsmokers breathing smoke-filled air.

Although politics plays a part in so many issues in our society, understanding the economic basis of political decisions can help one separate the reality from the rhetoric.

26

the economics of
Housing Prices and Controlling Growth

In many areas of the country, *growth* is a bad word. It's particularly a bad word for people who prefer to have their section of the country remain about the same as it's always been. Many attempts have occurred at controlling growth in the name of saving the environment, improving the ecology, and even preventing the depletion of our water supply (see Chapter 6). A little-known outcome of controls on growth, but one certainly not missed by many homeowners, is that when growth is controlled housing prices increase.

Housing prices throughout the United States increased quite dramatically in the 1970s and early 1980s. Much of this increase in the price of housing was attributed to the high inflation rates of those years. Inflation, and the anticipation of even higher inflation rates in the future, caused people to invest in real assets, such as land and housing. Also, during the late 1970s and early 1980s, prospective homeowners saw **real interest rates** actually dropping, even though market, or **nominal, interest rates** were rising. Real interest rates are defined as those rates of interest that exist when anticipated inflation is removed. For example, if mortgage interest rates are 13 percent and the rate of inflation is also 13 percent, then the real rate of interest is zero—a bargain. Also, investment in real estate meant a tax savings because most people were able to deduct mortgage interest payments from their income before paying taxes. In effect, when coupled with the low real rate of interest, the tax savings created a negative rate of interest. Favorable interest rates, which were due to high inflation rates, and the tax advantages of investing in real estate created an increase in the demand for housing during that period that rapidly pushed up housing prices.

California led the pack. The rate of increase for the price of homes in many California cities appeared astronomical. While it is true that California's population growth rate was above average during these years and that this growth in population added to the price-increase pressure, other factors were at work also. Other areas of the nation experiencing similar or even greater population increases, for example, did not see as large an increase in the average price of homes as occurred in some cities in California. Consider also that, from 1972 to 1979, the average selling price of a home in the Santa Barbara area increased from $36,192 to $129,982—an increase of 260 percent—while the general level of prices as measured by the Consumer Price Index rose only 75 percent during the same period.

How can such a dramatic *relative* increase in the price of housing be explained? Several economists at the University of California at Santa Barbara asked themselves this same question and studied the problem. Their conclusion was that, at least in part, the relatively higher increase in housing prices in Santa Barbara was due to an attempt to control growth by creating a water moratorium. In the mid-

1970s, various water districts in the Santa Barbara area imposed a *complete* ban on new water hookups. Others severely limited the number of new water hookups. The result was a reduction in the number of new houses that could be built. The homeowner groups that dominated the water district boards were responsible for a reduction in the number of new homes that were made available in the Santa Barbara area. The inevitable occurred. The demand for housing increased as population grew in California (the **demand curve** shifted outward to the right), whereas the supply of new housing increased very little (the **supply curve** stayed in about the same location). What occurred was that there were fewer new houses in the flow of housing; most purchases were of existing homes. The overall growth of housing in the area was notably reduced by the controls placed on water hookups. Effectively, the controls on water hookups meant controls on housing growth. Since housing in the area became more expensive, fewer would-be residents chose to live there.

Nearly 30 percent of the real increase in housing prices in Santa Barbara, in the time period under study, can be attributed to growth controls. The result was a housing "crisis"—a lack of "affordable" housing for many new entrants into the area or for many lower-income residents who had hoped to be able to own a home. Existing homeowners saw their houses increase in value more than they would have without the controls on water hookups.

SUMMARY

Growth controls, such as those in Santa Barbara resulting from the limitation placed on new water hookups, helped prices to rise 260 percent in that city during the late 1970s and early 1980s, while nationwide the average increase in the price of housing was only 75 percent. Effectively, the controls on water hookups limited the growth in the housing stock of Santa Barbara and pushed up prices of existing homes to levels "unaffordable" by many lower-income potential homebuyers and new entrants into the city.

DISCUSSION QUESTIONS

1. How is it possible to obtain a negative real rate of interest?
2. Who suffers most from housing growth controls? Why?

27

the economics of
Ecology
and Income
Distribution

There are few more unsightly aspects of the urban environment than the jungle of poles and overhead wires that foul the typical cityscape. When we extend the term "pollution" to include visual pollution, overhead wires are a prime candidate for inclusion in this category. The solution is to place them underground, and this process is going on in many cities around the United States.

Typically, the relocating of arterial wiring is paid for by a general rate increase; but in residential areas, it is not uncommon for the citizens of an area who want this change to form a Local Improvement District, develop a plan, and submit it to the appropriate body for approval. Usually the utility company pays part of the cost, and each lot owner pays a proportionate share of the rest (in Seattle, the ratio has been approximately 50–50). Placing wires underground in an already developed residential area is expensive, with the total amounting to sometimes several thousand dollars per lot. It is not surprising that this type of cost sharing has tended to restrict most underground wiring to higher-income areas. However, since the share paid for by the utility company comes from the general income received from everyone's rates, while benefits accrue to the upper-income groups, such projects reflect a redistribution of income from poor to rich.

Two options exist. We could insist that the lot owner pay the entire cost of placing wiring underground, in which case there would be no redistribution but also, probably, very little change. Or, we could let the utility company raise rates sufficiently to alter the wiring of the whole city, in which case everyone would pay. At a public hearing on the subject in Seattle a few years ago, the head of the local utility company testified that such a program stretching over a 10-year period would necessitate a doubling of electricity rates. A rate increase bears more heavily on the poor because the percentage of their income that goes for electricity is typically greater than the percentage for the rich. Thus the consequence is again to impose a greater relative burden on the poor than the rich. Is the case of underground wiring different in its effects on income distribution from other solutions to environmental problems?

Before we attempt to answer this difficult question, we reiterate a fact of which all readers should now be well aware. Every action has a cost. That is, every action involves some opportunity cost, whether or not this cost is explicitly stated or even understood by those incurring it. Since our world is one of limited resources, it is also a world of trade-offs. In the underground-wiring example, we can trade off higher electric rates (or smaller amounts of income to spend on other things) for beauty (no overhead wires). Beauty does not come to us free of charge. When it is realized that every alternative course of action involves certain sets of costs, then it is time to ask: Who will bear these costs? We have already seen what happened in one case. We can now discuss others.

Many citizens are attempting to have forest areas preserved as pure wilderness, arguing that we should preserve as much of our *natural* ecology (as opposed to that made by humans) as possible. Preserving wilderness areas involves costs and benefits. The costs include less forest area for other purposes, such as camping grounds and logging. Who bears these costs? People who like to camp (but not backpack) in the first case, and people who buy houses and other wood products[1] in the second.

Although the reader can easily understand the first case, the second may not be so obvious. Look at it this way. When fewer forest areas are used for logging, the supply of lumber is smaller than it would be otherwise.[2] With any given demand (schedule) the price of lumber will therefore be higher than otherwise, and houses become more expensive.[3]

Now for the benefits. Wilderness-area preservation offers benefits to those who like backpacking in the preserved area and to those who can enjoy fishing and hunting there. Benefits are also bestowed upon those who do not themselves backpack, hunt, or fish, but who would pay something to keep the wilderness for their children.

To determine what effect the saving of a natural ecology area has on the distribution of income, broadly defined, we have therefore tried to discover, as always, who bears the costs and who obtains the benefits. This is usually an empirical question, which can be answered only by examining relevant data. From limited studies that have been done, we can make a tentative conclusion about wilderness

[1]Or wood-product substitutes, for that matter.
[2]The supply schedule is farther to the left.
[3]Note that the same is also true for nonwood houses. If the price of wood houses is higher than otherwise, more people will substitute nonwood houses—and their price will be bid up (their demand schedule shifts outward to the right).

preservation. It has been found that backpackers are, in general, well educated and earn considerably more than the average. Thus the gains from that activity go to middle- and upper-income groups. As for who bears the costs, we know that campers (those with tents, trailers, and camper-trucks) are, on the average, less well educated than backpackers and earn considerably less. Hence, we are trading off recreation facilities used by lower-income people in favor of those used by higher-income people.

As for the increased price of housing resulting from less lumber, we know that the poor will suffer more than the rich, because housing expenditures are a larger fraction of the poor's budget.

We can easily take other examples. Question: Should the level of a dam be raised to provide more hydroelectric power, or should the virgin timber area around it be left a wilderness area for backpackers? As economists, we cannot answer the question. We can merely point out all of the costs and benefits associated with two (or more) alternatives. In this example, the costs (in ecological terms) of raising the dam level would be borne largely by actual and potential backpackers. The benefits would be lower electricity rates and/or the saving of resources that would have been needed to develop an alternative source of energy supply. If electricity payments represent a larger fraction of the income of the poor than the rich, raising the level of the dam might redistribute income from the rich to the poor. We say "might," because the income is redistributed only if the poor pay less relative to what they get.

There is, of course, a way of preserving our ecology without redistributing income.[4] The government could institute user charges for such things as wilderness areas and hunting preserves, setting them to cover the imputed opportunity cost of the resources being used. The totals col-

---

[4]But not without redistributing the use of resources.

lected could then be redistributed in a manner that would compensate those bearing the costs.

SUMMARY

Improving the environment is costly, and the benefits are seldom evenly distributed. We need to carefully analyze the distribution of the costs and benefits of alternative programs to see who benefits and who pays.

DISCUSSION QUESTIONS

1. Why aren't user charges imposed?
2. What would be the distributional consequences of installing air bags in all new automobiles?

28

the economics of
Black
Economic
Progress

For over 20 years, the federal government has attempted, by the legislative process, to reduce racial discrimination against blacks. How effective has this legislation been? Indeed, can equal opportunity be legislated?

In an attempt to answer these questions, two separate studies were undertaken a decade following the passage of the 1964 Civil Rights Act. Although these studies are now themselves over a decade old (they were both based on 1964–1975 data), they still render important insights into the problem of measuring black economic progress. One study was conducted by Richard Freeman of Harvard University. The other study, by James Heckman and Richard Butler of the University of Chicago, used essentially the same time series analysis and econometric techniques as Freeman.

Nonetheless, the conclusions reached were significantly different.

The authors all agreed that substantial black economic progress occurred between 1964 and 1975. The more spectacular gains had been made by black women: In 1964, the median wage or salary for black women was 58 percent of the median for white women; by 1975 it had risen to 97 percent. The status of black women's jobs had also improved substantially. For black male workers, the age and level of skill made an important difference in the degree to which they had caught up. In 1964, young black workers aged 20–24 earned 68 percent of what young white workers earned. By 1975, the figure was 85 percent. For older workers, the progress was slower. Comparable figures were 65 percent in 1964 and 70 percent in 1975. The most spectacular success for males had been among highly qualified blacks. Black professionals in 1964 earned 69 percent of what comparable whites did, but by 1975 this figure had gone up to 84 percent. Blacks with doctoral degrees and black graduates with bachelors' degrees in business appeared to do approximately as well in the mid-1970s as comparable whites.

On the basis of these findings, Freeman argued that the Civil Rights Act of 1964 had been a major factor in reducing discrimination and improving the lot of black wage earners. He concluded that the 1964 act shifted the demand curve to the right for blacks and used a mass of statistics to support the fact that it was this piece of legislation that altered the opportunity of blacks overall in American society. Heckman and Butler, on the other hand, concluded that the evidence did not show that there had been a shift to the right in the demand curve, but instead primarily a shift to the left in the supply curve. Their argument was that social expenditures on welfare in the late 1960s led to a reduction in labor force participation rates among low-wage workers—those most likely to participate in social welfare programs. Since there had been a much greater share of blacks in this low-wage group than whites, the consequence was to reduce relatively the supply of black workers in the labor force. According to Heckman and Butler, with a reduced supply of black workers at the low end of the scale, the relative wage of those blacks who remained in the labor force was clearly related. The key to their findings was that if market demand had shifted favorably for blacks, it should have resulted in an increase in the labor force participation rate. But, in fact, just the reverse happened; that is, the participation rate of blacks declined. Heckman and Butler believed that this finding was inconsistent with the shift in demand to the right that Freeman argued was a result of the Civil Rights Act. For Heckman and Butler, the most important source of improved well-being for blacks was the remarkable change in the American South due to improving school quality, industrialization, and out-migration from the South.

How far apart are these two positions? Heckman and Butler conceded that perhaps legislation had had some impact, particularly on young blacks, as mentioned earlier. And surely the improvement in schooling in the South and the somewhat greater readiness to employ blacks was, if not directly, at least indirectly tied to legislative activity. Nevertheless, the differences in these positions are important since they call into question the degree of effectiveness of direct legislation in prohibiting discrimination.

In the mid-1980s, the extent to which black economic progress can be attributed to antidiscrimination laws is still unclear. It is clear that for whites the poverty rate stood at 11.4 percent in 1985, while for blacks it was 31.3 percent. It is also clear that unemployment among black men is currently around 16 percent—more than twice that among whites—and for blacks under 20 the unemployment rate is nearly 45 percent. Hence, the problem of how a society can create equality of opportunity still remains.

SUMMARY

There appears to have been substantial black economic progress between 1964 and 1975. Two alternative reasons have been given. One is that the demand curve for blacks has shifted outward to the right because of the 1964 Civil Rights Act. An opposing view maintains that the supply curve of blacks has shifted to the left because welfare programs have reduced the labor force participation rate among blacks. Proponents of the second view argue that the major sources of improved black well-being are improved school quality, industrialization of the American South, and out-migration from the South.

DISCUSSION QUESTIONS

1. How would an increase in social welfare programs lead to a reduction in the labor force participation rate of minority groups?
2. How can you explain the greater relative progress made by black women, as compared to black men, in the marketplace?

29

the economics of
Educational
Vouchers

When the idea of educational vouchers first appeared in the 1970s, it seemed to be the ideal answer to the malaise that affected the school system. The idea was simple. Instead of giving money to public schools, with each child being assigned to a school (or alternatively occasioning outlays for private schools), vouchers would be given directly to families so that they could enroll children in schools of their choice. The idea had particular appeal for reformers who viewed the ghetto schools as an issue, since it offered parents alternatives to the poor education provided by the public school system. Catholics liked the idea because the vouchers would boost enrollment in parochial schools. Believers in the free market felt that it was the answer, since it provided a system of free choice in the educational world analogous to the market system in the economic world. The appeal of vouchers was that they would encourage competition, which would thereby shake up the school system and force it to be more attentive to the diverse needs that an educational system should satisfy. In short, the voucher system appeared to be the economist's ideal answer to a complex question.

But the voucher system met a storm of protest from inside and outside the educational establishment. Teachers viewed it as a way of union busting, administrators were afraid that they would lose control over budgets and appointments, and liberals felt that the flow of monies to sectarian schools would threaten the separation of church and state. Moreover, while the proposed plan provided freedom of choice, the voucher system would destroy the egalitarian principles of schooling since rich parents could supplement the amount of the voucher and send their children to more expensive schools, while poor parents could not. Thus the simple economics of the voucher system were placed in direct confrontation with the political economy of the system, reflecting the vested interests and views of groups that saw their values threatened.

Still, in the face of widespread opposition, the idea persisted and led the federal government to solicit school systems to try out the voucher system. However, since school systems usually were intransigent in their opposition, the federal government found it difficult to find a school system that would try the experiment. The little district of Alum Rock in California, however, was in poor financial condition, and its superintendent felt that any experiment could not help but ameliorate the multiple problems he faced.

What happened when Alum Rock tried the voucher system? Did more educational diversity result? Did the schools become more responsive to the will of the parents? Did the power of professionals wane? Competition among schools should have led to enrollment increases in programs that were appealing to parents and to unemployment for unpopular teachers who taught poorly. But the school professionals' first objective was to protect their jobs. Accordingly, it was immediately agreed that any teacher who left a voucher school for reasons associated with the experiment would be given priority in assignments to other schools. No one would be put out on the street. This decision eased things for unpopular teachers, but even for successful teachers the results were a mixed blessing. Although their schools received more tuition, the monies were spent for more teachers and untested materials, consequently increasing the everyday problems of teachers struggling with more planning, more meetings, and more colleagues. Professionals put a halt to extensive redistribution by imposing a ceiling on enrollments in schools. The result was that once a school reached its enrollment capacity, the spillover was, of necessity, returned to the less popular schools. School principals were particularly sensitive to any comparative testing that might have evaluated their relative performances; hence, comparative evaluations that would draw attention to differences and encourage parents to change schools were discouraged. In short, the program strayed a long way from the intentions of the original authors of the system.

Did parents respond to the new ability to make choices? Some did, and indeed by the third year approximately 18 percent of parents had chosen to send their children to schools outside the neighborhood. But the percentage was still small and reflected the passivity of most parents in the face of professionals. However, it would be a mistake to imagine that nothing did happen; in fact, greater diversity within the schools did emerge. Where before there had been a uniform curriculum, now there were Spanish-English bilingual programs, an arts and crafts minischool, and several open classrooms. In short, more innovation had taken place. Finally, it should be recognized that everyone knew that the Alum Rock experiment was a temporary one and that it would come to an end. Therefore, the degree to which it reflected the experience that might have taken place under permanent conditions was very limited indeed.

What can be learned from the Alum Rock experiment? First of all, by and large parents did not exercise much more choice than before. The power of school administrators and professionals emerged undiminished and, indeed, may have increased. On the other hand, there is no doubt that the experiment promoted diversity among schools and encouraged further experimentation. Nevertheless, the entrenched position of teacher and administrator groups led the experiment far from the original intentions of those who wished to impose the conditions of the market on the school system.

What would happen, though, if the voucher system were used on a larger scale, in a larger school district, and on a more permanent basis? Supporters of the voucher system still maintain that it would be a large step toward the elimination of the discrimination against minorities and the poor that takes place in the public school system. Such discrimination occurs because parents in high-income groups can "afford" either to locate in residential areas where good public schools are located or, if they choose, to send their children to private schools. Both options are often nonexistent for the lower-income groups. Proponents of educational vouchers claim that if the $3000 or so spent on each child in the public school system were given instead to families in the form of vouchers to be redeemed at the school of their choice, it would help to equalize opportunities among income classes and to improve the school system. Increased competition among schools for students would force school administrators to curtail violence, involve parents in curriculum formation, and control costs more effectively.

In short, the argument for educational vouchers remains today essentially what it was in the 1970s. The difference, current supporters say, is that while the idea was too novel for the 1970s, its time has come. And it is apparent that interest in the voucher system is far from dead. A 1985

Gallup poll showed that 59 percent of nonwhites and 43 percent of whites favor educational vouchers. And, very recently, Secretary of Education William J. Bennett proposed a similar method for financing remedial education, whereby parents of students requiring such instruction would be given vouchers for $600 a year. These vouchers could be used at either private or public schools to help finance such remedial education.

But what in theory is one thing often in practice turns out to be quite another. Whether one evaluates the Alum Rock experiment as a success or a failure, it did show how the simple economics of choice applied to an institutional structure can be modified by the realities of political economy, in which vested interests inevitably will alter the way the market is permitted to work.

SUMMARY

Under a system of educational vouchers, competition will cause a larger variety of schooling environments to exist. If public schools were allowed to coexist with private schools under the educational voucher system, public schools would have to provide services of equal quality to private schools. Not surprisingly, public school officials have routinely fought the implementation of an educational voucher system.

DISCUSSION QUESTIONS

1. In most metropolitan areas, a wide variety of nursery schools exist. Some specialize in art, some in dance, some in scholastic training, and others in sports. Once the child reaches kindergarten or first-grade age, however, the choice of schools becomes much less varied. Why?
2. Although educational vouchers were first proposed 30 years ago by economist Milton Friedman, they

have never, as yet, taken hold in this country. How can you explain the lack of success of what would seem to be an equitable method of financing education for American school children?

30

the economics of

Income Distribution and Government Programs

As has been done in many countries, our government has instituted programs for helping sectors of the economy where aid seems to be needed. In most cases, the implicit aim of these various programs is to effect a redistribution of income.

As pointed out in Chapter 27, all programs to improve or maintain our environment involve both costs and benefits. This is true of any government program. If we are to understand the actual, as opposed to the avowed, redistributional aspects of any governmental policy, we must fully assess the range of costs and benefits. Also, once again, we must determine empirically who bears these costs and benefits.

Let us examine the redistributional effects of the farm

program. The obvious intent of this program is to maintain farmers' incomes at a level that society feels is acceptable (that is, not "too" low). The questions to be asked are: (1) Does the program fulfill that purpose? Who reaps the benefits? And (2) how is the program paid for? Who incurs the costs?

To answer the first question, those farmers who produce and sell the most crops will receive the most income from the government in the form of deficiency payments and other subsidies (see Chapter 4). In general, this would indicate that benefits from the farm program are proportional to farmers' incomes, since those with larger farms usually have higher incomes. Because roughly 80–90 percent of all agricultural crops marketed are produced by about 10 percent of U.S. farmers, it is evident that the farm program is not benefiting mid-sized and smaller farmers—as it was intended to do. Indeed, a recent study by the Department of Agriculture indicates that the vast majority of income and price support payments go to the largest and wealthiest farmers. And only 18 percent of farm-program payments go to the neediest farmers. It is the farmers in the latter group who are leaving the business of agriculture in droves for other income-producing alternatives. During 1985 and 1986, approximately 100,000 farmers quit the business of farming because they could no longer meet their costs.

The farm program also tips the scales in favor of wealthy farmers in another way. This is because higher-income farmers have more access to knowledge of legal procedures that can help them maximize their benefits from the farm program. Currently, for example, farm-program regulations specify that no person can receive more than $50,000 in deficiency payments for any one crop. But the regulations also allow a "person" to be a corporation, a partnership, or a trust—as well as an individual farmer. Technically, as long as any of these legal entities (1) has a legal interest in the land or crop, (2) participates in management, and (3) is liable for losses as well as profits, then such an entity is entitled to deficiency payments. In order to increase their payments from the government to more than this $50,000 maximum, many farmers have taken advantage of this rule and formed two or more legal entities within the same family. According to Agriculture Department officials, it is common to find farms splitting into 4 to 10 or more legal units over a period of years. In one case, a rice farm in California was divided up 56 ways—and received nearly $1.5 million in income subsidies.

Who bears the cost of the farm program? In general, we can say that taxpayers do to the extent they contribute to government revenues.

After looking at the benefits and costs of our farm program, one can only conclude that its effect is apparently to redistribute income from relatively lower-income groups to relatively higher-income groups. Of course, this assertion would be invalidated if it could be shown that the poor pay proportionately lower taxes toward governmental expenditures than do the rich.

Turning now to our income tax system, let us consider how certain tax deductions redistribute income. An individual paying off a home mortgage is allowed to deduct the interest payments. This is an incentive for home ownership, since buyers benefit by not having to apply their tax rate to that amount of income. Ms. A, whose annual mortgage interest payments equal $1000 and whose tax rate is 15 percent, will gain $150 in income that does not have to be handed over to the government. Splendid! But consider the case of Mr. B., who earns twice the salary of Ms. A and is in the 33 percent tax bracket. For the $2000 he paid out as interest this year, which he deducts from his income tax, he saves $660. The rich individual with a mortgaged home has benefited more than a less rich person in the same situation and far more than a poor individual whose tax rate is zero, or than anyone who has no mortgage payments on which to receive concessions.

We have already considered the ways in which income is redistributed by laws that make prostitution and narcotics illegal. In both cases we can say that, since information is more costly for illegal goods and services, in general those who can afford to pay more (the wealthy) receive a "better" product that those who are poor.

We can also recall the questions of rent controls. If laws controlling rents are effective, they establish a price below the market-clearing price. Dealers in rent-controlled apartments therefore look for nonpecuniary returns when renting. Who is a better risk, a person who makes $30,000 per year or a person who works off and on for about $10,000 a year? Under rent control, will the landlord rent to a welfare recipient or to the daughter of a city council member? At the same rental price, the landlord will probably rent to the latter, since she is more likely to make her rent payments regularly.

All of these examples are given to illustrate the need to examine the distribution of the costs and benefits of government programs and to decide whether they actually redistribute income in the intended direction. To the contrary, it appears that many policies tend to favor the rich at the expense of the less rich. However, this assumption must be verified anew for any prospective program.

SUMMARY

An analysis of many government programs shows that they do not benefit poor people, as generally intended. For example, any farm program that involves income supports and the like benefits farmers in proportion to their output. Poor farmers are, by definition, those who do not have large output. Therefore, richer farmers benefit the most from government farm programs. As a general proposition, many government programs tend to benefit others than the very poor in our society.

DISCUSSION QUESTIONS

1. Discuss a government program that favors the poor.
2. On balance, what are the distributional consequences of federal government tax and expenditure programs?

31

the economics of
Smoking

Twenty years ago smoking existed everywhere; indeed, it was something of a status symbol to smoke. Television ads and movies showed the heroes and heroines dangling cigarettes from their mouths. But since then the image of the smoker has changed dramatically. Smokers are now hailed by many as self-indulgent, self-destructive polluters who are inconsiderate of the effect their smoke has upon others nearby. By 1985, 85 percent of nonsmokers thought that smokers should refrain from smoking when others are present, a Gallup poll showed. The same poll showed also that, although smokers may be self-indulgent and self-destructive, they are not all inconsiderate of others: 62 percent of the smokers in the survey agreed with the nonsmokers that smokers shouldn't inflict their smoke on third parties.

The beginning of this dramatic change in attitudes toward smoking can be dated from the 1964 Surgeon General's report, which made it clear that smoking is harmful to one's health. As the link between lung cancer and smoking became more firmly established, increasingly stern labels were required on cigarette packages to warn consumers of the health hazards caused by smoking. In recent years, the focus has been broadened to include the adverse health effects of smoking on "passive smokers," nonsmokers who are continually exposed to smoke-filled air either at home or in the workplace. One study showed that 5000 Americans die every year as a result of second-hand smoke, and a recent Japanese report concluded that wives of heavy smokers had an 80-percent higher risk of developing lung cancer than women married to nonsmokers. Heart disease has also been connected to passive smoking. Whether smoking physically harms nonsmokers to any significant degree, though, is still a debated question; vehement proponents of the rights of smokers can cite several scientific studies that have been unable to establish such a relationship between "passive" smoking and significant harmful health effects. But there can be no doubt that smoking can be irritating and obnoxious for the nonsmoker and that, whether they want to or not, nonsmokers are forced to breathe the polluted air created by smokers in numerous situations.

Smoking is a classic case of an externality, one in which it would be appropriate for the smoker to compensate the nonsmoker for the discomfort felt—according to the efficiency standards of the economist. Or, in the absence of compensation, the correct policy might be to impose rules and regulations that prevent the smoker from being able to irritate the nonsmoker. Why doesn't the federal government simply ban smoking? An economist is in no position to answer that question. The economist can point out the costs and benefits involved and measure the externalities involved, but ultimately the issue becomes one of political economy. And the government's position is not that unequivocal. What the government does with its left hand—

the Department of Health and Human Services and the Surgeon General's Report, which has resulted in a heavily subsidized publicity campaign to prevent smoking—is countered by its right hand—the Department of Agriculture's subsidies to the tobacco industry. The approximately 500,000 growers of tobacco in the United States are prevented from competition by laws that do not allow increased acreage and that provide a prohibitive tax of 75 percent on all tobacco grown on unlicensed land. The result is to provide monopoly returns to those growers fortunate enough to have been in on the beginning of this subsidy (which started some three decades ago).

There's still more to the right hand of government. Federal tax receipts from the sale of cigarettes in 1986 approximated $5 billion, and this doesn't include receipts from import duties on tobacco and tobacco products. Clearly, some parts of the federal government feel that they have a great deal to gain from the continued use of tobacco. So does the subsidized farmer in the American South, who is receiving direct returns from the monopoly granted to tobacco growing and supported by the Department of Agriculture. And—it goes without saying—so, too, do the 55 million Americans who call themselves smokers and who spend over $30 billion a year for tobacco products.

There can be no doubt that if smoking were discovered for the first time today, it would be put in the same class as cocaine, heroin, and dangerous drugs and considered something that should be outlawed by society. But smoking grew up to be a national craze in an era when it coincided with a prestige value, and it still retains much of that aura for young people. And obviously smokers are voters, too, as are tobacco growers and the growing legions of antismokers. As a result, it is not surprising that the politics of smoking should lead to contradictory roles in government—where the left hand works to prohibit smoking and the right hand to promote it.

State and local governments, however, are not faced

with such a dilemma. And pressures from health organizations and antismokers have led to a spate of legislation in recent years, at the state and local levels, prohibiting smoking in public areas. By 1986, 39 states and numerous localities had ordinances against smoking on public transportation and in public places. In the same year, Mayor Ed Koch of New York proposed one of the most stringent antismoking laws ever. If it passes, the only havens in that city for smokers will be private residences, bars, and hotels and motels and a few other areas excluded from the ban. Antismokers won another victory recently when the University of Chicago banned all retail sales of cigarettes on campus, notwithstanding the $50,000 loss in revenues that this may cause. Private firms across the nation, when providing a nonsmoking area would prove too costly, are increasingly resorting to hiring nonsmokers as a solution to personnel problems brought about by the battle between nonsmokers and smokers. Even at the federal level the "left hand" may prove to be the stronger. The Nonsmokers Protection Act of 1986, recently introduced into Congress, would, if passed, ban smoking in federal buildings throughout the United States, even in the proverbial smoke-filled rooms and corridors of Congress. And, as if to console smokers, in a study released in 1986 Surgeon General C. Everett Koop—himself a vehement campaigner against smoking—made existing legislation against smoking look pale before what has happened in other countries in the past. In seventeenth-century China, he pointed out, anyone found possessing tobacco could be beheaded.

SUMMARY

Problems related to smoking are both internal and external. Internal problems involve self-infliction of such diseases as lung cancer. External problems involve polluting the air that others breathe. Since air is common property, there is no *a priori* reason to argue that nonsmokers have more rights to clean air than smokers have rights to pollute the air. A decision to prohibit smoking imposes a cost on smokers; a decision to allow smoking imposes a cost on nonsmokers. The argument is symmetric because air is common property. The federal government for years has maintained an equivocal position on smoking—supporting the tobacco industry on the one hand and subsidizing publicity campaigns against smoking on the other. Legislation prohibiting smoking in public areas at the state and local levels, however, as a result of pressure from health groups and antismoking consumers, is effectively placing the cost of the externality of smoke-polluted air on smokers.

DISCUSSION QUESTIONS

1. Is there a similarity between the analysis of smoking and the analysis of the use of wilderness areas by motorcycle riders?
2. How would you compare the problem of air pollution created by smokers to that of pollution created by industrial plants?

Glossary of Terms

Aggregate demand: The dollar value of planned expenditures for the economy on all final goods and services per year.

Aggregate supply: The total dollar value of all final goods and services supplied by firms to the market economy per year.

Antitrust legislation: The enactment of laws that restrict the formation of monopolies and regulate certain anticompetitive business practices.

Bond: An interest-bearing certificate issued by a government or a corporation. This type of security represents debt.

Capital: All manufactured resources, including buildings, equipment, machines, and improvements to land.

Capital gain: The positive difference between the purchase price and the sale price of an asset. If a share of stock is bought for $5 and then sold for $15, the capital gain is $10.

Cartel: A group of independent industrial corporations, usually on an international scale, that agree to restrict trade to their mutual benefit.

Commodity Credit Corporation: A government agency that "lends" farmers an amount of money equal to the support price of crops times the amount offered as collateral for the loan.

Common property: Property that is owned by everyone and therefore owned by no one. Examples of common property resources that have historically been owned in common are air and water.

Common stock: A security that indicates the real ownership in a corporation. A common stock is not a legal obligation for the firm and does not have a maturity. It has the last claim on dividends each year and on assets in the event of firm liquidation.

Competition: Rivalry among buyers and sellers of outputs, or among buyers and sellers of inputs.

Complementary goods: Two goods are considered to be complementary if a change in the price of one causes an opposite shift in the demand for the other. For example, if the price of tennis rackets goes up, the demand for tennis balls will fall; if the price of tennis rackets goes down, the demand for tennis balls will increase.

Constant quality unit: A unit of average, or standard, quality by which all units are measured.

Consumer Price Index: A statistical measure of a weighted average of prices of a specified set of goods and services purchased by wage earners in urban areas.

Cutthroat, or predatory, pricing: Pricing goods below marginal cost until competitors are forced to leave the market.

Deficit: The negative difference between inflows and outflows, or, more specifically, between income and expenditures; the term is often applied to government and called a government budget deficit.

Demand curve: A graphic representation of the demand schedule. A negatively sloped line showing the inverse relationship between the price and the quantity demanded.

Demand schedule: A set of pairs of numbers showing various possible prices and the quantities demanded at each price. This schedule shows the rate of planned purchases per time period at different prices of the good.

Discounting: A method by which account is taken of the lower value of a dollar in the future compared to a dollar in hand today. Discounting is necessary even after adjustment for inflation because of the tradeoff between having more goods tomorrow if we consume less today.

Distribution of income: The way income is distributed among the population. For example, a perfectly equal distribution of income would result in the lowest 20 percent of income earners receiving 20 percent of national income and the top 20 percent also receiving 20 percent of national income. The middle 60 percent of income earners would receive 60 percent of national income.

Dumping: A term used to describe a practice whereby a business firm charges high prices domestically to subsidize losses incurred by selling at lower prices abroad in order to obtain a share of a foreign market.

Economic good: Any good or service that is scarce.

Economies of scale: Savings that result when output increases lead to decreases in long-run average costs.

Elastic demand: A characteristic of a demand curve in which a given percentage change in price will result in a larger percentage change in quantity demanded, in the opposite direction. Total revenues and price are inversely related in the elastic portion of the demand curve.

Elasticity of demand: The degree to which buyers will be sensitive and respond to a change in price.

Equilibrium, or market-clearing, price: The price that clears the market where there is no excess quantity demanded or supplied. The price at which the demand curve intersects the supply curve.

Expansion: A business fluctuation in which overall business activity is rising at a more rapid rate than previously, or at a more rapid rate than the overall historical trend in a particular country.

Externalities: A situation in which a benefit or a cost associated with an economic activity spills over to third parties. Pollution is a negative spillover, or externality.

Free good: Any good or service that is available in quantities larger than are desired at a zero price.

Generic drugs: Drugs marketed under the generic name of the drug, rather than under a brand name. Penicillin, for example, is a generic drug; Ampicillin is a brand name for the same drug. As long as a pharmaceutical firm holds a patent for a brand-named drug, that drug cannot be sold generically.

Income effect: The change in purchasing power that occurs when the price changes of one good that is purchased, other things being held constant.

Income elasticity of demand: The percentage change in the quantity demanded divided by the percentage change in money income; the responsiveness of the quantity demanded to changes in income.

Inelastic demand: A characteristic of a demand curve in which a given change in price will result in a less-than-proportionate change in the quantity demanded, in the opposite direction. Total revenue and price are directly related in the inelastic region of the demand curve.

Inflation: A sustained rise over time in the weighted average of all prices.

Inside information: Any kind of information that is available only to a few people, such as officers of a corporation.

Investment: The summation of fixed investment and inventory investment. Any addition to the future productive capacity of the economy.

Labor: Productive contributions of individuals who work, involving both thinking and doing.

Law of demand: A law that states that the quantity demanded and price are inversely related—more is bought at a lower price, less at a higher price (other things being equal).

Law of supply: A law that states that a direct relationship exists between price and the quantity supplied (other things being equal).

Liability: Anything that is owed.

Marginal costs: The change in total costs due to a change in one unit of production.

Market-clearing, or equilibrium, price: The price that clears the market when there is no excess quantity demanded or supplied; the price at which the demand curve intersects the supply curve.

Minimum wage: A legal wage rate below which employers cannot pay workers.

Models, or theories: Simplified representations of the real world used to make predictions or to better understand the real world.

Money supply: A generic term used to denote the amount of "money" in circulation. There are numerous specific definitions of the money supply. The narrowest is simply currency in the hands of the public plus demand deposits held only in commercial banks. This has been labeled the M1A money supply by the Federal Reserve System.

Monopolist: A single supplier.

Monopolistic competition: A market situation in which a large number of firms produce similar but not identical products, in which there is relatively easy entry into the industry.

Monopoly: A firm that has great control over the price of a good. In the extreme case, a monopoly is the only seller of a good or service.

Monopsony: A single buyer.

Negative externality: A cost associated with an economic activity that is paid by third parties. Pollution is a negative externality.

Nominal interest rate: Defined as the rate of exchange between a dollar today and a dollar at some future time. For example, if the market, or nominal, rate of interest is 10 percent per year, then a dollar today can be exchanged for $1.10 one year from now; the market rate of interest.

Oligopoly: A market situation in which there are very few sellers and in which each seller knows that the other sellers will react to its changes in prices and quantities.

Opportunity cost: The highest-valued alternative that must be sacrificed to attain something or satisfy a want.

Parity: A concept applied to the relative price of agricultural goods. The federal government has established parity by using a formula in which the price of agricultural goods was compared with the price of manufactured goods during the period 1910–1914. A parity price would give farmers the same relative price for their products (compared to what they buy) that they received during the period 1910–1914.

Predatory, or cutthroat, pricing: Pricing at below marginal cost long enough to drive competitors from the marketplace.

Preferred stock: A security that indicates financing obtained from investors by a corporation. Preferred stock is not a legal obligation for the firm and does not have a maturity, but pays a fixed dividend each year. It has preferred position over common stock, both for dividends and for assets in the event of firm liquidation.

Price elasticity of demand: The responsiveness of the quantity demanded for a commodity to a change in its price per unit. Price elasticy of demand is defined as the percentage change in quantity demanded divided by the percentage change in price.

Price elasticity of supply: The responsiveness of the quantity supplied of a commodity to a change in its price per unit. Price elasticity of supply is defined as the percentage change in quantity supplied divided by the percentage change in price.

Price support: A minimum price set by the government. To be effective, price supports must be coupled with a mechanism to rid the market of "surplus" goods that arise whenever the supported price is greater than the market-clearing price.

Profit: The income generated by selling something for a higher price than was paid for it. In production, the income generated is the difference between total revenues received from consumers who purchase the goods and the total cost of producing those goods.

Public information: Any kind of information that is widely available to the public.

Random walk: This refers to the situation in which future behavior cannot be predicted from past behavior. Stock prices follow a random walk.

Real interest rate: The rate of exchange between goods and services (real things) today and goods and services at some future date. The nominal rate of interest minus the inflation rate.

Recession: A period of time during which the rate of growth of business activity is consistently less than its long-term trend, or is negative.

Resource: An input used in the production of goods and services desired.

Saving: The unspent portion of a consumer's income, or the difference between a consumer's income and his or her consumption expenditures.

Scarcity: A reference to the fact that at any point in time there exists only a finite amount of resources—human and nonhuman. Scarcity of resources means that nature does not freely provide as much of everything as people want.

Shortage: A situation in which an excess quantity is demanded or an insufficient quantity is supplied; the difference between the quantity demanded and the quantity supplied at a specific price below the market-clearing price.

Social costs: The full cost that society bears when a resource-using action occurs. For example, the social cost of driving a car is equal to all the private costs plus any additional cost that society bears (e.g., air pollution and traffic congestion).

Stock: The quantity of something at a point in time. An inventory of goods is a stock. A bank account at a point in time is a stock. Stocks are defined independently of time although they are assessed at a point in time; savings is stock.

Subminimum wage: A proposed minimum wage of $2.50 an hour specifically to apply to summer and temporary workers. A subminimum wage law, according to proponents, would result in lower teenage unemployment rates.

Subsidies: Negative taxes; payments to producers or consumers of a good or service. For example, farmers often get subsidies for producing wheat, corn, or peanuts.

Substitution effect: This occurs when a change in the price of one economic resource or good causes a shift in the demand for another (substitute) economic resource or good in the same direction as the price change.

Supply curve: The graphic representation of the supply schedule; a line showing the supply schedule, which slopes upward (has a positive slope).

Supply schedule: A set of prices and the quantity supplied at each price; a schedule showing the rate of planned production of each relative price for a specified time period, usually one year.

Supply-side economics: A popular approach to economics in the early years of the Reagan administration ("Reaganomics"). Supply-siders maintain that an increase in the tax rate will cause a decrease in the amount of work (and income) within the economy; conversely, a decrease in the tax rate will cause an increase in the amount of work (and income) within the economy.

Surplus: A term for an excess quantity supplied or an insufficient quantity demanded. The difference between the quantity supplied and the quantity demanded at a price above the market-clearing price.

Tradeoff: A term relating to opportunity cost. In order to get a desired economic good, it is necessary to trade off some other desired economic good in a situation of scarcity. A tradeoff involves making a sacrifice in order to obtain something.

Union: An organization of workers that usually seeks to secure economic improvements for its members.

Value of marginal product: The change in total revenues that results from a unit change in a variable input; also equal to marginal physical product times marginal revenue, or MPP × MR.

Variable costs: Costs that vary with the rate of production. They include wages paid to workers, the cost of materials, and so on.

Index